Self-Talk

Change your mind, change your life

Workbook

Sally H. Hall

COMPERIO PRESS

Self-Talk
Published by Comperio Press
©2018 Sally H. Hall

First edition February 2018
Revised July 2018

ISBN 978-0-9995129-0-6

All Scripture, unless otherwise indicated, are taken from the New American Standard Bible® (NASB), Copyright © 1960, 1962, 1963, 1968, 1971, 1972, 1973,1975, 1977, 1995 by The Lockman Foundation. Used by permission. www.Lockman.org. Scripture marked (NIV) are from New International Version, International Bible Society 1973, 1978, 1984, are used by permission. Scripture marked The Message© 1993, 1994, 1995, 1996, 2000, 2001, 2002. Used by permission of NavPress Publishing Group. Scripture taken from the Amplified® Bible (AMP), Copyright © 2015 by The Lockman Foundation. Used by permission. www.Lockman.org. Scripture marked (NLT) are taken from the Holy Bible, New Living Translation, copyright ©1996, 2004, 2007, 2013, 2015 by Tyndale House Foundation. Used by permission of Tyndale House Publishers, Inc., Carol Stream, Illinois 60188. All rights reserved. Scripture marked (GNT) are from the Good News Translation in Today's English Version - Second Edition Copyright © 1992 by American Bible Society. Used by Permission.

Bolded words and parentheses () within Scripture quotations reflect the author's added emphasis.

All rights reserved. With the exception of quotes or brief excerpts used in social media, articles, review or promotion, no part of this book may be reproduced or transmitted in any form or by any means, electronic or mechanical, including photocopying and recording, or by any information storage or retrieval system, except as may be expressly permitted in writing by the publisher. Requests for permission should be sent to Sally H. Hall via sallyhhall.com.

What Others Are Saying

If you are wondering how to make it in this crazy world, **Self-Talk** *is for you. With media clips, personal illustrations and simple Biblical truths, Sally Hall will lead you step-by-step toward an understanding of why you struggle with your relationship to yourself, the world, and God. She will show you where to look for answers to questions you've never dared to ask; and in the process, you will discover insights that will bring sanity to your life. You will love this self-help Bible study for changing the way you think through changing your all-important* **Self-Talk**.

Jan Silvious
Author, Speaker, Life Coach
Big Girls Don't Whine
Fool-proofing Your Life
Courage for the Unknown Season
jansilvious.com

Sally Hall has taken the good news of Jesus Christ and applied it with laser-like focus to the conversations that are swirling in all of our minds. **Self-Talk** *is Sally's own courageous journey with the God who transforms hearts, held out as an encouragement for all of us to "be transformed by the renewing of our minds." While many authors aim at this, Sally connects us better than most to the rest of that verse: "that by testing you may discern what is the will of God, what is good and acceptable and perfect." Romans 12:2. May God use this book to set many people free from the shackles of deception and into the amazing freedom that Jesus Christ gives!*

Tim Ackley
MA Counseling
Ordained Minister
Lead Pastor Cornerstone Church
cefetoday.com

Words—You simply cannot get away from the words you speak to yourself and others or the words others speak to you and about you. But, what you can do, is become more aware of the impact your words have. This is exactly what Sally Hall will help you recognize and understand as you unpack her recent book, **Self Talk**. *Through Sally's personal journey, scripture, and practical application, you will discover the truth about who you are and where your identity lies. You will embrace your God-given worth, learning to positively and powerfully walk it out to a watching world.* **Self-Talk** *will transform your body, mind, soul, and spirit by replacing lies you may believe with straight up truth!*

Jessie Seneca
Author, Speaker & Leadership Trainer
Friendship, Sisters for a Journey
Raising Girls Diaper to Diamond
moreofhimministries.org

Self-Talk —hmmm—do I need this study? Well, just look at several of the chapter titles. "Life is a wild ride"—an understatement for sure. "It's a crazy world"—definitely true. "There's good news"—I need some good news right now. "You are God's masterpiece"—Me? How? "Prepare your mind for action"—sounds encouraging. Conclusion: I need "***Self-Talk***." Do You?

Gail Maddox
Bible Teacher

I have the privilege of working with many authors and have a veracious appetite for reading in general, but this can sometimes leave me with a super critical spirit! I was so pleasantly surprised and excited when I read ***Self-Talk***. It hit the "nail on the head" with its insight and understanding. Sally Hall has done a wonderful job of laying out strong truths about how we should view ourselves and where we often go wrong. I found myself almost giggling out loud at some of her examples and then feeling deeply convicted at the next. In the end, I was left with one permeating thought: "I wish I had read this when I was in my 20's!" This is a must-read for all of us because no one totally escapes the negative self-talk that is so easy to listen to in today's world.

Sandy Ellingson
Executive Strategist
servestudios.com

There's an old saying, "sticks and stones will break my bones, but words will never hurt me" ... oh boy, that is a lie. Even as children we tend to accept and believe the negative things people say, add them up for years on end, and the result is a deeply wounded and confused individual. I love that ***Self-Talk*** gives you the opportunity to tear down that wall by replacing negative words with the truths of God's Word. I am looking forward to sharing the ***Self-Talk*** Bible study with women who desperately desire to know the One who calls them His beloved.

Brenda Brown
Volunteer Supervisor
the-wellhouse.org

One of the greatest enemies you will ever face is yourself. We believe what we tell ourselves is truth, and if that truth is negative, you may find that you have very little self-worth. You not only have to change your inner dialogue from "I'm ugly" to "I'm beautiful", but you have to find a real truth in what you are telling yourself. You have to change your perspective. ***Self-Talk*** will allow you to discover how God sees you and who he made you to be. God has a plan for each of us and through meditating on Scripture you can start to reflect on the positive and dispute the lies you tell yourself.

Buffie Bogue
M.S. Kinesiology/Sport Psychology;
Behavior Analysis;
Child Development and Family Studies

Dedication

How I thank God for the people He used and how He used them. Each contribution was priceless and made this work a reality. First and always to my husband Tom for his continued support and encouragement to do the things God puts on my heart to do. Then, to a group of very godly and dedicated people who contributed by graciously and faithfully praying, editing, working through, piloting, reading, and re-reading this workbook. Gail, Brenda, Sandy, Chrystal, Jenny, Donna, Yolanda, Chelsea, Beth, Jes, Buffie, Joseph, Ellyn and Pastor Tim. I am so grateful for your wisdom and prayers. A special thanks to Heather and Bridget for their help on photos and graphics. Many thanks to Sondra for using her amazing talents and abilities to edit and design the workbook. To my social media friends and family who saw my posts, selected the sub-title and cover design, gave great feedback on some of the content, and prayed—you are all amazing. Thank you! To God be the glory.

Contents

Getting Started	9
Introduction	11
#1 Life is a Wild Ride	13
#2 Get a Grip on the Strong Bar	25
#3 It's a Crazy *World*	39
#4 There's Good News	55
#5 You are a Masterpiece	71
#6 Walking and Working in the *World*	99
#7 The Truth About Trouble	125
#8 Prepare Your Mind for Action	145
Conclusion	165
Appendix	167
Notes	171

Getting Started

This 8-week, Bible-based, self-help workbook is designed to help you:
- Examine your self-talk,
- Discover why you tell yourself what you do, and
- Determine if what you are telling yourself is the truth.

In the process, you'll find the tools and develop the life skills needed to mentally manage the emotional ups, downs, twists, and turns of life.

Below are a few things you'll need as you work through *Self-Talk*.
- Pen or pencil
- Highlighter (if you like using highlighters)
- Notebook for additional notes
- Time

Before you start:
- Commit to completing the workbook.
- Look at your calendar:
  - Block out 8 or more weeks.
  - Set aside sufficient time each week to do the work. It could take you an hour or more to work through each chapter. If you find it difficult to work through an entire chapter at one sitting, consider dividing chapters into 15 to 20-minute segments. Sometimes stepping away to process the questions is the best approach to giving honest and thoughtful answers. Don't rush through the workbook but try to take no longer than two weeks to complete each chapter. If you realize it is going to take you longer than 8 weeks to finish the workbook, be sure to schedule the extra time you'll need on your calendar. Doing these few things will help you finish the workbook.
- Identify a workspace. Make sure you can get comfortable and be free of distractions.
- Think about what you should not write in the workbook. Be careful about writing names or personal details in your workbook. If you do, protect yourself by making sure your workbook is not accessible for others to read.

Individual and group use:

- Be sure to check out the resources section at sallyhhall.com[1] for videos, audios, and other resources that will enhance your self-discovery.
- Write out your answers to the questions in the spaces provided throughout the workbook. If you run out of space, write additional answers and thoughts in a notebook.
- All the passages from the Bible we'll examine together are included in this workbook below each reference. Each reference shows you the book, chapter, and verse from the Bible being quoted. Unless otherwise noted, the New American Standard Bible version is used.
- Before many of the references are instructions to look for and mark certain words. Watch for and follow the instructions, as the markings will help you answer the questions that follow each reference.

Group discussion guidelines:

This workbook is designed for individual use. However, group discussion questions and a group leader's guide can be found at sallyhhall.com in the resources section.

Introduction

"You are the most influential person in your life because you talk to yourself more than anyone else."
-Paul Tripp[1]

The above quote by Paul Tripp begs the question: "What am I telling myself?"

The movie *Inside Out*[2] is about a young girl named Riley. She had been uprooted from her Midwest life and moved to San Francisco. Her emotions of *Joy, Fear, Anger, Disgust*, and *Sadness* were depicted as characters or voices in her head guiding her through this difficult and life-changing event. You can find a free preview of *Inside Out*[3] in the resources section of my website at sallyhhall.com[4].

I encourage you to take the time to watch the movie or the movie clip because throughout the movie you'll see *Joy, Fear, Anger, Disgust,* and *Sadness* running around inside Riley's head, trying to make sense out of what was happening in her life. I have found that as my *Joy, Fear, Anger, Disgust*, and *Sadness* battle it out in my head, it can be like mental ping-pong or like riding an emotional roller coaster. Also, there are many more emotional characters running around in my head that would not be Disney movie material.

Just like Riley, as we take in life around us, our self-talk shapes how we feel, what we think, believe, and ultimately what we do! We are the most influential people in our lives because we do talk to ourselves more than anyone else! Oh, the things I've told myself only to find out later I had no idea what I was truly doing to myself. So, when one of those pictures with words showed up on my Facebook feed stating, "Don't believe everything you think," I would share it adding hashtag truth! One of my husband's favorite sayings is "You don't know what you don't know!" #truth.

We believe what we tell ourselves is the truth. But, is it? And, what is truth anyway? Can truth change or is it absolute?

This 8-week, Bible-based, self-help workbook is designed to help you examine your self-talk, discover why you tell yourself what you do, and determine if what you are telling yourself is the truth. In the process, you'll find the tools and develop the life skills needed to mentally manage the emotional ups, downs, twists, and turns of life.

#1 Life Is a Wild Ride

Words and relationships power the ride

Please take the time to read the Introduction and Getting Started. Also, be sure to watch the free preview of Inside Out[1]. You can find it in the resources section of my website at sallyhhall.com.

The unexpected twists, turns, ups, and downs of life evoke a variety of emotions, all of which are normal and are also very powerful. As you watch *Inside Out*, imagine the voices of the emotions *Joy, Fear, Anger, Disgust, Sadness*, and *others* running around crazily in your mind.

Emotions are powerful because whether riding up or down, our emotional self-talk during the ride becomes what we believe about our circumstances, ourselves, others, life, and the world in general. Just like Riley from the movie *Inside Out*, what you and I tell ourselves and believe during the wild ride of life ultimately determines the direction of our lives. An old proverb cautions us to: "Be careful how you think; your life is shaped by your thoughts" (Proverbs 4:23 GNT).

We all know this is true, but the ride is so wild, fast, and overwhelming that hanging on is all we can do. Examine our self-talk? Hardly. Until we just want off the ride because we realize things are far too wild and crazy, or we are worn out from just hanging on.

If that's you, then it's time to stop and think about "what" you are thinking! Specifically, to examine and explore your own self-talk.

Let's begin by looking at how words and relationships power the wild ride of life.

You have probably already experienced that *positive* words and relationships inspire, encourage, and strengthen you. At these times, your confidence rises. You go high and fast in the emotion of *Joy*. Other times, *negative* words and relationships strip you of your confidence and send you flying down the track while the emotions of *Fear, Anger, Disgust,* and *Sadness* are screaming or running around wild in your head.

What others say *to* you.

Earlier this year, I was blessed to visit with a dear friend. How wonderful it was getting caught up and spending time together. Since last seeing her, she had changed her hairstyle. When I mentioned how much I loved it, she shared with me that it was the first time in her life she had no bangs. Fascinated, I asked why. She explained to me that her mother had told her at a very young age that she needed to wear bangs because her forehead was too big. This dear friend is now in her 50's, but her mother's words still ring true in her head to this day.

Years ago, I had friends that were sharing with me the fun they had on a shopping trip. One of the gals tried on a blue top that all the others thought looked fabulous on her and made her eyes and hair pop. When they encouraged her to buy it, she said no to the blue top. She explained she never wore blue. Apparently, someone she dearly loved told her she didn't look good in blue. She believed what was said and told herself blue would never be in her wardrobe.

Recently, I was asking a young man I know if he'd always had a beard. He shared with me that he first had a beard in high school. It was at the same time he was madly in love with his high school sweetheart. When he decided to shave off his beard, she proceeded to tell him how ugly he looked without it. He grew his beard back and vowed he'd always have a beard. He's now in his forties and has stayed true to his word.

The opposite of these scenarios could also be true. Someone that matters to us tells us we look great without bangs and it is no bangs—forever! Or, that blue is our color and so blue is the color we wear the most. "I love your clean-shaven" face, so clean-shaven it is!

Take a few minutes to think about and write down some examples of how *positive* words spoken to you have shaped what you believe about yourself and how you talk to yourself. (Examples: great personality, beautiful hair, leader, blue is your color, wonderful parent, so organized, prayer warrior, physically fit, good cheek bones, you've got skills, etc.).

CHAPTER 1: LIFE IS A WILD RIDE

- What *positive* words have shaped how you think and what you believe about yourself?

Positive or *negative*, words have power.

Let me share some personal examples of how *negative* words powered and made for a wild ride in my life. These are just a few highlights that had all the characters of emotion in my head running around talking crazy and in many ways trained my brain:

- I moved to Atlanta when I was 12, and a young 12 at that. I still enjoyed playing with dolls. Evidently this is something city girls didn't do, and so I was made to feel like a silly girl who didn't measure up or fit in. Because I had never experienced such hatefulness or rejection, I tried to take my life. Fortunately, I was unsuccessful, told my parents, and they put me in a school where I could mature at my own pace.

- I was told at 19 by my high school sweetheart and first husband (of less than a year) that he loved me but thought of me as a sister. This made me feel like I didn't measure up as a bride, a wife, and a woman. More rejection. That message and the voice of the rising women's movement had my emotional characters of *Sadness, Fear, Anger,* and *Disgust* confused and talking crazy for years.

- "Truth" speakers told my second and still husband of 40+ years and me that we must have done something very wrong and sinful not to be blessed with children. Wow, I guess the bottom line of my life was that I didn't measure up to God and He was rejecting me too. It was a decade of *Sadness* before I knew what to do with those words.

   These were defining moments in my life that shaped what I believed about myself and how I talked to myself. In writing this book, I discovered that *negative* situations and words say to me "rejection" and "you don't measure up." I have just shared my default self-talk. How about you? What is your default self-talk?

Take a few minutes and write down 1 to 3 personal examples of defining moments in your life when *negative* words, spoken into your life, have shaped what you believe about yourself and how you talk to yourself (possible default self-talk).

- What defining moments impacted you **negatively**? Using my examples, be as brief and general as possible.

- As a result of these **negative** situations and words, what is your possible default self-talk? Record your initial thoughts below.

CHAPTER 1: LIFE IS A WILD RIDE

What others say *about* you.

If you have ever been the object of gossip or, worse, slander, then you certainly understand the power of words. Thinking shaped. Lives impacted. Emotions evoked. At least one life devastated. No examples are necessary. Gossip and slander, or as some would call it, sharing information, is extremely powerful in shaping what others think about you. Words are powerful.

Let's talk further about that sharing of information—perhaps not as far as gossip or slander. People are having a conversation in which information about you, your life, and your activity is being discussed. What someone else might know about you could be based solely on what they learn about you during that conversation. They get another person's version of you. Perceptions, opinions, and determinations about you, your life, your work—whatever, is shaped having never heard your version of you. If those perceptions about you are wrong, your wild ride goes from fast to perhaps furious.

- What do you tell yourself when perceptions, opinions, and determinations about you, your life, your work—whatever, are wrong? Write your thoughts below.

Like me, you might be realizing that in these situations your default self-talk kicks in—big time. For me, the voices of "rejection" and "you don't measure up" keep me from thinking objectively. Certainly, what others say about me powers the wild ride. Honestly, in these situations, my default self-talk powers the ride even more so than what others say about me.

SELF-TALK: Change your mind, change your life

What the world says *to* and *about* you.

When I was a young woman growing up in the 60's and 70's, a popular song was *I Am Woman Hear Me Roar*[2] by Helen Reddy and the most watched commercial was Enjoli[3]. For your viewing pleasure, videos of both can be found in the resources section of my website at sallyhhall.com. Please take time to watch them as the messages are powerful.

All these years later, the lyrics to both the song and the commercial are still in my mind.

- Growing up, what popular songs or commercial lyrics shaped your thinking?

I remember "hearing" I was supposed to look like a combination of Barbie[4] and Twiggy[5], which is impossible. For other words that shaped my thinking about womanhood, check out these popular messages from my era displayed on buttons.

My generation spoke loudly about sex, drugs and rock and roll, about not trusting government, racial pride, self-sufficiency, and equality for all people of Black and African descent. At the same time I was hearing all those messages, the church in general was silent. Go figure!

CHAPTER 1: LIFE IS A WILD RIDE

As a young woman of the "me generation,[6]" it was hard wrapping my mind around womanhood as taught and modeled by my mother versus what I was learning in school and from the world. Each concept was mixed and often contained conflicting words or messages. Because the messages I heard said life was all about "me," I took a little from here and a little from there all for the sake of the emotion *Joy*. In the end, I came up with what felt right to and for me at the time.

Just in case you haven't noticed, let me point out that *Joy* is the most favored emotion. She wins out most of the time. I am all for keeping *Sadness* in her circle (I am referring to scenes from the *Inside Out* extended movie clip).

Each decade and generation have a voice—new messages. For example, the sexual revolution, down with marriage, the rise of drugs, everyone gets a trophy, LGBT, and same sex marriage. Yes, each generation has a voice, and that voice shapes our thinking and fuels the wild ride of life. Take a minute and write down the messages and words of your generation.

- What are the messages and words of your generation?

Positive, negative, true, or false—words are powerful.

Relationships speak.

Several months ago, I had coffee with a dear young woman who had just ended a decade-long relationship. Her statement "I just want to be loved" still echoes in my heart. However, the relationship was so verbally and physically abusive and damaging that she is left feeling unloved and unworthy of love. I kept hearing her say "if only I were…" It was so reflective of her self-talk. It appeared to me that *Sadness* and *Fear* ruled.

Harsh words, actions, and rejection from those who have full access to our hearts and our ride is at warp speed. The voices of our every emotion begin to scream and run wild.

I have another friend who experienced much physical and verbal abuse as a child from not just one person, but multiple people who should have been protecting her. She has a wonderful relationship with her husband who is loving and affirming, but at times *Joy* is nowhere around. While *Shame* is not a character in the movie *Inside Out*, the emotional character *Shame* is real for my dear friend. Unfortunately, *Shame* is real for many of us. I think *Shame* might have an iron fist if you know what I mean.

We will have many different types of relationships in our lives. Some intimate as in full access to our hearts. Others will be merely acquaintances, and still others will be distant. We will have family, friends, teachers, schoolmates, bosses, co-workers, teammates, and neighbors. When the relationship is good, *Joy* jumps. Up, up, up we go—riding high and fast. Our self-confidence is boosted. When the relationship is *negative*, we fly down, down, down, and crash. The emotional characters of *Sadness, Fear, Shame*, or others will rule at those times.

I remember a T-shirt I saw recently. The message on the front said, "Stay home. It's too peoply out there." *Negative* relationships can send us into hiding and cause us to have endless conversations in our heads with ourselves. If you just understood what I said, then you understand the power of relationships.

Words and relationships power the ride because they fuel our emotions. All day long you process verbal and non-verbal messages. Some *positive* and some *negative*. False information, helpful information, and too much information. Up, up, up you go. Down, down, down you can fly. But here's the thing. Whether riding up or down, your self-talk during the ride becomes what you believe about yourself, others, your life, and the world in general. Your self-talk determines your behavior, actions, your future, and everything.

What are you telling yourself?

My experiences of ups and downs have certainly messed with my mind and altered the way I view myself and the world around me. The wild ride has messed me up, stunted my growth, propelled me forward, and taken me higher and lower than I ever imagined.

Negative words, shattered dreams, acts of rejection, betrayal, failures as well as broken and lost relationships. They have all shaped my thinking and trained my mind. Yes, I have had many *positive* words spoken into my life, a few dreams realized, and have experienced loving relationships.

But, here's the strange thing. The flying down, the downside of emotions, words, and relationships, has impacted my self-talk as much, if not more than the *positive*. Yes, *Joy* has jumped, but *Sadness, Fear, Disgust, Shame, Guilt,* and the others are right there talking, talking, talking—reminding, reminding, reminding. Often, holding me back, holding me down, and sometimes beating me up. What's up with that?

- Which do you believe has had the greater influence on your self-talk? Is it *negative* emotions, words, and relationships or the *positive* emotions, words, and relationships?

Now might be a good time to suggest that we can't always believe everything we hear, think and tell ourselves! But, more on that later!

For now, as we continue to explore our self-talk, let's focus on our body image. Make a list below of the *negative* words or messages that shape what you believe and tell yourself about the way you look. (Examples: big nose, pear shape, big forehead, beady eyes, ugly feet, hair color, beard, big hands, large pores, fat, skinny, double chin, etc.).

- What is your **negative** body image self-talk?

When *negative* words and relationships come your way, and those *negative* emotions rise, what do you tell yourself? Let's call this our default self-talk.

Review the following list and check anything on the list that you currently tell yourself.

Negative self-talk

- ☐ This is all my fault.
- ☐ I am a bad person.
- ☐ This wouldn't have happened if I were prettier or smarter or thinner or...
- ☐ There must be something wrong with me.
- ☐ I am unlovable.
- ☐ I am ugly.
- ☐ I am not enough.
- ☐ This is not fair.
- ☐ I am a failure.
- ☐ I knew if they knew me they wouldn't like me.
- ☐ Nothing good ever happens to me.
- ☐ I am worthless.
- ☐ I am stupid.
- ☐ God must hate me.
- ☐ God doesn't love me.
- ☐ If God is so good why...
- ☐ I don't measure up.
- ☐ I don't want anything to do with a God that could let this happen.
- ☐ I will never love again.
- ☐ No one will ever love me.
- ☐ I am so ashamed.
- ☐ I can never forgive myself.
- ☐ If only I were _____, this would be different or wouldn't have happened.
- ☐ I can't.
- ☐ I won't.
- ☐ I give up.
- ☐ I don't care.
- ☐ I can't do this.
- ☐ It's not worth it.
- ☐ I can't trust anyone.
- ☐ I must have done something wrong for all this to happen to me.
- ☐ I'm being punished.
- ☐ More rejection.
- ☐ I am never going to _____ again.
- ☐ I deserve this.

Add *negative* self-talk not included in the above list:

CHAPTER 1: LIFE IS A WILD RIDE

If you have made it this far in the workbook, great job. Understanding what we tell ourselves and why is critical.

Negative words, physical abuse, acts of rejection and betrayal, shattered dreams, the loss of loved ones, relationships, health, etc. all shape our self-talk. Fill in the blank—life, death and everything in between. Life is a wild roller coaster of a ride. Up, up, up we go. Down, down, down we fly. The wild ride can send us flying and out of control.

Here's another thing about our wild ride and where we'll go next. We need to hang on, but what are we hanging on to? The last time I rode on a roller coaster, there was a big, strong metal bar that came across and securely held me. The wilder the ride, the stronger my grip was on that strong bar.

There is a line from a poem entitled "Life is a Roller Coaster[7]" by Lewis Bunting that says:

> *"Some bars you trust, some bars you don't,*
> *and you sometimes get it wrong*
> *but there will always be that one strong bar*
> *that's held you all along."*

Life is a wild ride! You need to hang on, but what is that one strong bar that's holding you? Let's go there next.

#2 Get a Grip on the Strong Bar

Up, up, up you go. Down, down, down you fly. Hang on! But, what are you hanging on to?

"Emotional roller coasters tend to emphasize the lows, tend to be more affected by the low, by the dip in an emotional roller coaster than when you are at the peak."
-Rush Limbaugh[1]

You may or may not be a Rush Limbaugh fan or not even know who he is, but this quote certainly describes my wild ride on the emotional roller coaster of life! As I have already mentioned, my self-talk testifies that the dips in the ride have affected me more than the peaks. But, what am I telling myself? The better question is, am I telling myself the truth?

Perhaps as you have explored your self-talk, you also realized the dips in the wild ride of life—caused by negative words and relationships—have impacted you more than the peaks. As a result, are you telling yourself the truth?

What is truth?

Some would say, and I would agree, that my self-talk has proven that I believed truth was relative to me and my circumstances. I often made decisions based on whatever felt right or was comfortable to me in that situation. Or, I would make decisions based on what I thought would bring me relief and find joy. *Joy always wants to jump!* Whatever "felt" right became my truth.

For example, my truth about what it meant to be a woman was a mix of what my mother and the church told me, the voice of my generation, what the world of TV, movies, and magazines were saying, and what I thought "felt right" when I combined them all.

A while back, I was visiting with a young woman. We were talking about the movie, *Is Genesis History*[2]? It's a movie that looks at Genesis, the first book in the Bible. Together with science and history, it seeks to determine if the Bible is an accurate account of creation. As we discussed the movie, she started processing with me what she had heard about the big bang theory, what she'd read in Genesis, what she'd learned in school, what others had told her, and what she was trying to determine in her mind was true about God and the book of Genesis.

You could almost see the wheels turning in her head as she tried to make it all fit into something she could wrap her mind around and accept. Her conclusions about God and creation were a mix of all the information acquired about God.

As I sat there and listened to her and watched her process out loud, I thought to myself. "I do the same thing." In every situation, I take all the words I hear from others and the words I tell myself and try to come up with what makes sense and "feels right" to me. What about you?

Words are so powerful because they shape what we think about ourselves, others, the world around us, and even what we believe about God. Paul Tripp's quote is quite appropriate.

> *"You are the most influential person in your life because you talk to yourself more than anyone else."*

Which also begs the questions: "What do we tell ourselves and how did we determine it as truth?" I've shared with you how I have often determined truth. I also shared how my friend determined what she believed. Now it's your turn.

- Explain how you determine what is the truth.

Opinions, attitudes, and actions can be influenced and, therefore, change. If truth is situational and based on what "feels right," or what I think or believe is right, then what happens when things change or no longer "feel right?" What happens when we discover that what we determined and told ourselves was a lie rather than truth? We are often left emotionally exhausted and damaged. That's what!

Now is the appropriate time to stop and ask this question:

- Is it possible to know that you know that you know what is true of you no matter what is going on to and around you?

Remember the extended clip from *Inside Out*? Well, imagine my very own *Joy, Fear, Anger, Disgust*, and *Sadness* (as well as a few others) all running around in my head trying to make decisions based on whatever "feels right" or is comfortable. Again, the visual projected from my head would not be a cute Disney movie. But, the Disney movie is a good visual. At one point in the movie, *Sadness,* having read all the mind manuals, helps *Joy* navigate the maze of long-term memory. Did you catch that? *Sadness* had read the mind manuals. Wait! During all that craziness and running around, they could have stopped and referred to the mind manual. Going to that mind manual earlier could have certainly saved them a lot of chaos and turmoil.

Is it possible there's a mind manual we can and should be referencing?

Yes! There is a mind manual for life. Who knew?

God's Word as absolute truth.

Please don't zone out on me. Give me this chapter. As you fly up and down through life, you need to know for yourself if there is a strong bar of absolute truth on which to hold. Truth that will not and does not change—ever, no matter what.

Life is a wild ride, and there is a strong bar of truth on which to hold.

God, in His Word, has a very clear standard for us. Standard means "something set up and established by authority as a rule for the measure of quantity, weight, extent, value or quality."

What this means is that truth is not relative to my circumstances. Wow, *that* truth was an eye opener. No matter what my experiences tell me, no matter what I tell myself or what the emotional characters in my head are screaming, no matter what others tell me, and no matter what is going on in society or culture, I can and should grip the strong bar of absolute truth.

How do you know I didn't just tell myself this in my head? Let me explain. I was desperate for answers. What I was telling myself in my head wasn't working. I didn't have a clue about the power of emotions, words, and relationships or life and how these things were shaping my thinking. I couldn't put the pieces of life together in a way that made any sense. Things were not turning out as I had been led to believe they would, or expected they would, or hoped they would. *Joy, Fear, Anger, Disgust*, and *Sadness* were wild and crazy in my head! I was totally missing the point of life. I wondered if I had I missed an important life memo or something.

> No matter what my experiences tell me, no matter what I tell myself or what the emotional characters in my head are screaming, no matter what others tell me, and no matter what is going on in society or culture, I can and should grip the strong bar of absolute truth.

Consulting with myself was not working. On any given day, the truths in my head about my life kept changing based on how I felt and what I thought was right. Mix in what I was hearing from those around me and the world, and wild doesn't come close to describing the ride. Make it stop!

What I thought was true wasn't holding me. There was no strong bar of absolute truth. What I thought was right wasn't working. I was desperate to know if there was a way to make sense out of this wild ride called life. I was desperate for answers.

In my quest for answers, I decided to go to God's Word to see if and what He had to say about truth in His Word. Here's what I discovered.

- ☐ God means what he says. What he says goes. His powerful Word is sharp as a surgeon's scalpel, cutting through everything, whether doubt or defense, laying us open to listen and obey. Nothing and no one is impervious to God's Word. We can't get away from it—no matter what. (Hebrews 4:12-13 - The Message)
- ☐ God watches over His Word to perform it. (Jeremiah 1:12)
- ☐ God's Word is **inspired** or God-breathed. This is pretty amazing, so read the insight box. All scripture is inspired by God and profitable for teaching, for reproof, for correction, for training in righteousness; so that the man of God may be adequate, equipped for every good work. (2 Timothy 3:16-17)
- ☐ God's Word is very pure. (Psalm 119:140)
- ☐ God's Word is eternal and stands firm in the heavens. (Psalm 119:89 - NIV)
- ☐ God exalts or magnifies His name together with His Word. (Psalm 138:2)
- ☐ The sum of or all of God's Word is true. (Psalm 119:160)
- ☐ God's Word is truth. (John 17:17)
- ☐ God's Word—truth—is our only weapon against the lies of the world and the evil one. (Ephesians 6:10-17)
- ☐ No prophecy of Scripture is a matter of one's interpretation—no prophecy was made by an act of human will, but men moved by the Holy Spirit spoke from God. (2 Peter 1:20-21)
- ☐ Whatever was written in earlier times was written for our instruction, so that through perseverance and the encouragement of the Scriptures we might have hope. (Romans 15:4)

To learn more about various Bible translations, original languages, and how we got the Bible, visit the American Bible Society[5] website.

- Did you know God said all of the above (and more) concerning His Word in His Word?
- Go back and put a check mark next to any of above truths that are new to you, stand out to you, intrigue you, or challenge your thinking.

The original language of the New Testament was Koine Greek.

Inspired (Theopneustos 2315) in the original language means to breathe or blow; prompted by God, divinely inspired by God.

Zodhiates, Spiros: *The Complete Word Study Dictionary: New Testament*, electronic ed. Chattanooga, TN:AMG Publishers, ©1992, 1993, 2000, Strongs G2315

Perhaps, like me, you've heard all the comments about God's Word. Comments like, "It's old, outdated and not relevant, men wrote it, it's been translated and interpreted, and it's not meant to be taken literally." But, I had to admit, some of these comments go totally against what we just read that God says about His Word in His Word. For example, God, in His Word, says *all* Scripture is God breathed and that *all* of His Word is true. Paul, the writer of 2 Timothy, was moved by God to write the words *all*. Whether looking at the original text or current translations, the word *all* means *all*. Do I believe *all* of God's Word is absolute truth? If I can pick and choose from God's Word what I believe is truth, and you can pick and choose from God's Word what you think is truth, then we have no absolute truth. If we have no absolute truth, then it seems to me we have no truth at all.

- Write down any opinions, questions, hesitations or reservations you have about God's Word being absolute truth.

Our opinions, questions, and thoughts are important because what we believe shapes our thinking and determines how we live our lives. When coming to our conclusions about whether God's Word is absolute truth, have we given God equal opportunity to speak for Himself about His Word?

Maybe you have this all figured out, but remember I was desperate for answers, I needed answers. When you've tried everything and nothing works, it sometimes moves you to sit down and read the manual rather than winging it. So, I sat down and started reading the manual for life—God's Word. I mean really reading it looking for answers, like it is truly a manual for life.

At first, I would try to find the word of the moment or quick fixes to get me through the ups and downs. It was all about me. I'd do Bible studies about whatever trauma or drama I was experiencing. But eventually, I started wanting to know more about God, what He thought about my trauma or drama, to understand why He wrote the book (manual), and to hear what He had to say about life. Yes, especially my life!

I discovered in Genesis that God showed Himself as Creator. Just a few verses into the very first book of the Bible (Genesis), He shares the beautiful story of how on six consecutive days He created everything—the heavens, earth, man, all the living creatures on the earth and, finally, a woman. Surely, the grand finale. These first few pages in God's book reveal how He planned and prepared for them, but also for us. From the very beginning, there was a relationship between God and man. Did you catch that? A relationship.

Drawn into their relationship, I continued to read and was amazed. God planted a garden for man. Can you imagine? Then God placed the man (Adam and Eve) in the garden. God gave them the garden He had planted to cultivate and keep. After God formed every beast of the field and every bird of the sky, He brought them to Adam so that he could see them and name them. I want to see *that* movie!

The more I read, the more I discovered God is intimately involved in the lives of people. These intimate relationships intrigued me. Book after book, name after name that I can't pronounce—are people. God interacted with people. God in intimate relationships with people. God revealed Himself in personal and incredible ways.

In the pages of His book, we can learn a lot about the wild ride of life and see how emotions, words, and relationships power that ride. And, guess what? We aren't the first people to question God or ask if His Word is absolute truth. It's so interesting what people have in common. Since the beginning of time (Genesis, the first book of the Bible), questions and doubts about God and His Word have been asked. Questions and doubts like:

Did God really say that?
Surely that's not what God means?
God must be holding out on me!

In the beautiful garden, God planted a tree called the tree of knowledge of good and evil. Below is what God instructed Adam and Eve about this tree. As you read, note the instructions God gives.

All the passages from the Bible we'll be exploring together in this workbook are included below each reference. Each reference shows the book, chapter, and verse from the Bible that is being quoted. Unless otherwise noted, the New American Standard Bible version is being used.

Read Genesis 2:16-17

¹⁶…from any tree of the garden you may eat freely; ¹⁷but the tree of knowledge of good and evil you shall not eat, for in the day that you eat from it you will surely die.

- Just for the fun of discovery, use the space below to write out the instructions God gives. As you do, make sure to write down exactly what God says and not your version of what God says.

Read Genesis 3:1-7

¹Now the serpent was more crafty than any beast of the field which the LORD God had made. And he said to the woman, "Indeed, has God said, 'You shall not eat from any tree of the garden'?" ²The woman said to the serpent, "From the fruit of the trees of the garden we may eat; ³but from the fruit of the tree which is in the middle of the garden, God has said, 'You shall not eat from it or touch it, or you will die.'" ⁴The serpent said to the woman, "You surely will not die! ⁵For God knows that in the day you eat from it your eyes will be opened, and you will be like God, knowing good and evil." ⁶When the woman saw that the tree was good for food, and that it was a delight to the eyes, and that the tree was desirable to make one wise, she took from its fruit and ate; and she gave also to her husband with her, and he ate. ⁷Then the eyes of both of them were opened, and they knew that they were naked; and they sewed fig leaves together and made themselves loin coverings.

Here is where it gets interesting and makes it so "peoplely out there" for us. Looking at what you just read in Genesis 3:1-7, answer the following questions.

CHAPTER 2: GET A GRIP ON THE STRONG BAR

- According to verse 1, how is the serpent described?

- Based on verses 1 and 4 through 5, what did the serpent say to Eve?

- How does what the serpent said to Eve line-up with what God said in Genesis 2:16-17 (page 32)? Write out below any similarities or differences.

- How did the serpent's questioning of God's Word impact Eve's thinking? Check out Genesis 3:6 (page 32). Write out below how she responded.

- According to Genesis 3:7 (page 32), what happened after they ate the fruit?

Sitting here looking in on their story, don't you just want to say: "Oh Eve, don't believe everything you think and hear." She added to what God said, the serpent came along questioning what God said, and the rest is history. No, we aren't the first people to question or doubt God or His Word, take someone else's word for God's Word, or add to God's Word.

Get a grip on the strong bar of God's Word, truth or any old lie will do!

Like Eve, we see and feel, and are so often ruled by emotions. There will be times when the ride of life is so wild and "feels" so bad, we'll think God is holding out on us. We'll wonder if God's book is the real deal and if we can believe it's absolute truth because some of those truths won't "feel right," will seem hard, and make us believe God is holding out on us.

As we continue to explore our self-talk, it's important to understand these thoughts and emotions because life is a wild ride. You and I will get a grip on something.

- What is or has been a strong bar that you grab on to and that holds you during wild and difficult times?

- If you don't have a grip on the strong bar of absolute truth (God's Word), then how will you know if you are telling yourself the truth?

- If you don't know whether you are telling yourself the truth, then any old lie will do. True or false?

What are you telling yourself about God's Word and why?

- Write out below what you believe about God's Word, why you believe it, and how you came to that decision.

We'll grab on to and hold the truth, or we'll grab on to and hold lies. If we don't know there is absolute truth, then how will we know the difference? Like me, if you leave it up to yourself to decide what is true or not, you will always decide based on whatever "feels right" or comfortable because the emotional character of *Joy* inside your head always wants to joyfully jump.

I am suggesting that if you don't take up what I am calling the manual for life—God's Word—and read it for yourself, you will never know for sure what's in it, what it says about you or if what it says works. You will never really know God for yourself. You'll never know for sure if God is holding out on you because you'll only and always assume He is.

You'll only have a mixed-up version of life and God because you will only pick and choose what you *think* works and is right or true.

Consider this: It's a historical fact that Jesus was crucified, buried, and raised from the dead. Research it for yourself and you will find there were eye witness reports. After Jesus was crucified, buried, and God raised Him from the dead, He was walking along the road and came upon two men. They did not recognize Jesus when He asked them what they were discussing. So they began telling Him all that had happened concerning Jesus. When they finished, here is what Jesus said to them.

Read Luke 24:25-27

25 …O foolish men and slow of heart to believe in all that the prophets have spoken! 26 "Was it not necessary for the Christ to suffer these things and to enter into His glory?" 27Then beginning with Moses and with all the prophets, He explained to them the things concerning Himself in all the Scriptures.

- Based on verse 25,
  Who was Jesus speaking to and how does he describe their heart?

  Slow of heart to do what?

- According to verse 27,
  Beginning from where did Jesus explain things to them?

  What did He explain to them?

Remember the book of Genesis is where we read about Eve. Well, guess who wrote Genesis? Moses! To the slow of heart to believe, Jesus started with Moses (Genesis), all the prophets, and then in all the Scriptures explained the things concerning Himself.

The same books that comprise the Old Testament today (Genesis through Malachi) are the same books that made up the Old Testament during Jesus' time and from which he would have explained all things concerning Himself. I love this. Why? The fact that Jesus accepted the Old Testament and taught from it confirms to me that every book written by men was inspired by the Holy Spirit of God. Not convinced? Do the research for yourself! Also, go back and read what God Himself says about His Word on page 29.

- How does what you have been told about God's Word or believe about God's Word line up with what God Himself says about His Word on page 29. Write out your thoughts below.

Perhaps you aren't convinced God's Word is absolute truth. Then, let me encourage you to start in Genesis. As you read, ask God to help you get to know Him personally by showing you how He relates personally to each person through the ups and downs of their life. Talk about wild rides and the power of words and relationships.

You'll be amazed at what you'll see and learn about God, His character, standards, and Word. These are true and sure and for you and me! Oh, and by the way, look for Jesus!

- How would you describe your relationship with God's Word? There is no right or wrong answer. Just be honest. Check one:

    ☐ Intimate and the final. (God's inerrant Word is the final and sufficient authority for all my life. As such, I am consistently in the Word of God discovering and personally experiencing truth in a way that comforts, satisfies, and transforms my thinking and life. It is a priority relationship.)

    ☐ Acquainted and taken into consideration. (God's Word is considered in my decision making. I do attend or have attended Bible studies, listen to sermons, and sometimes personally experience truth in a way that comforts and convicts me. If my life gets too busy, I will neglect my relationship with God's Word. It is not a priority relationship.)

CHAPTER 2: GET A GRIP ON THE STRONG BAR

☐ Distant and irrelevant. (When I hear God's Word it sometimes moves me, but not in a way that changes my thinking/life or causes me to want to become better acquainted, develop an intimate relationship, or to make a priority relationship.)

- What will your strong bar be?

If you don't have a grip on the strong bar of truth (God's Word) then how will you know if you are telling yourself the truth? If you don't know if you are telling yourself the truth, then any old lie will do.

Getting a grip on the strong bar of truth—God's Word—allows me to *"live expectantly, trying to tame my own ambitions, so they won't obscure what God has for me. I live passionately, knowing that God's will for me is not a passing phase or an emotional high. And I live meaningfully, knowing that God has a call on my life that is stronger, deeper, and richer than anything that came before."*
                    Dale Hanson Bourke from her book *Second Calling*[5]

Life is a wild ride! Words and relationships power the ride and shape what we think, believe, and do. Positive words and relationships send you up, up, and *Joy* jumps for joy. Negative words and relationships send you flying down and hanging on for dear life. But, what are you hanging on to? Get a grip on the strong bar of truth because not only is life a wild ride, but it's a crazy *world* out there! Let's talk about it.

#3 It's a Crazy World!

Understand and take courage

When you think about the *world*, your life, and future in it, or the lives and future of your children, or perhaps your grandchildren, what do you say to yourself? What is your self-talk? Do you expect things to be happily ever after, or the good life as you see it in your mind, or whatever success looks like (the career, house, car, dog, 2.5 kids), that people are good, or the *world* is a beautiful place?

- What do you tell yourself about the *world*, life, and the future? Write out your answer.

These days, I find myself thinking of the *world* as crazy. I find myself saying or thinking "This is crazy!" I listen to the news, and "crazy" comes to mind often. I see things when I am out in public, and "crazy" comes to mind. I wonder, "Has the *world* gone crazy?" Sometimes I'm the crazy one or talking crazy to myself! Let me clarify. When I say crazy, I mean full of cracks and flaws, and totally unsound. I am saying things are "way off."

I wasn't expecting life to be a wild ride or the *world* to be crazy. My answer to what I tell myself about the *world*, life, and the future was life, liberty, and the pursuit of happiness. My future was the happily ever-after life! A life where *Joy* always jumps and *Sadness* stays in her circle (from the *Inside Out* extended movie clip). Nope, not here. There are happy times in this life when *Joy* jumps, but there are things about this crazy *world* you need to know because a crazy *world* makes you full of cracks and flaws, and unsound!

My wild ride in this crazy *world* was like being on the biggest, most scary roller coaster ride in the dark with nothing to hang on to! But, when I finally got my grip on the strong bar of God's Word, I discovered God, in His Word had much to say about this *world* in which we live, the people in it, and why it's so crazy. I am sharing this with you because I was in my 40's before I discovered these truths. Why hadn't someone told me there was so much in the manual of God's Word about the *world* in which we live? Maybe they had, and I just wasn't listening or didn't want to hear it. But surely, had I known, I could have been better prepared mentally and emotionally for the wild ride of life in this crazy *world* than I was.

Crazy, cracked, flawed, and totally unsound

Imagine my surprise when I discovered that the word *world* is mentioned 57 times in the book of John (New Testament). Desperate for answers, I took the time to read the book of John, circled every reference to the *world*, counted the references, and then made a simple list of what I learned. What I discovered changed how I view the *world*. It changed my thinking. It changed what I was telling myself about the *world*.

As I read the book of John and got to the end of Chapter 20 (verse 31), I saw with my very own eyes why John wrote the book. It says right there in black and white that all had "been written so that you may believe that Jesus is the Christ, the Son of God; and that believing you may have life in His name." God, through the Holy Spirit, moved in the heart of John to write that book for me (and you), and God preserved it for us so we'd have it. Alrighty then. I had to go back and read it again!

While reading John, I marveled at account after account of Jesus' life and His relationships and interactions with people. The *world* was a crazy place then too. Everywhere Jesus went there was an abundance of hurting, sick, demon possessed, dying, and dead people needing help, hope, healing, freedom, and life. Honestly,

CHAPTER 3: IT'S A CRAZY WORLD!

the needs were overwhelming. Everywhere Jesus went, so went His disciples. They slept, ate, worked, lived, and ministered to people. Together! This account of Jesus' life also reveals the impact His words and relationship had on the thinking and behavior of His disciples. Jesus rocked and changed their *world*.

The account of Jesus' relationship with His disciples is important, so let me repeat the last two sentences. "This account of Jesus' life also reveals the impact His words and relationship had on the thinking and behavior of His disciples. Jesus rocked and changed their *world*." This is a great example of the power of words and relationships!

Jesus' words to them and their intimate relationship with Him certainly shaped what they thought, believed, and did. It not only changed the direction of their lives but how their lives impacted the *world*.

As I read along in John, I noticed that the closer Jesus got to the events of the cross and His death, the more He talked to His beloved disciples about the *world*. His last words to them were about the *world*. His last prayers for them were about the *world*. Forty-one times in three chapters alone Jesus references the *world*. What in the *world*?

About a week before Jesus was crucified and died, he rode into Jerusalem on a donkey, greeted by people who waved palm branches and who shouted Hosanna. Afterward, Jesus told his disciples this about the *world*.

Read John 12:31 (Jesus speaking)

Now judgment is upon this world; now the ruler of this world will be cast out.

- In this verse Jesus mentions the *world* twice. What are the two things Jesus wants us to understand about this *world*?

What? Judgment? A ruler of this *world*? Oh boy, this is when my *Fear, Anger, Disgust*, and *Sadness* start screaming "This is not good. This can't be good!"

Read John 16:33

These things I have spoken to you, so that in Me you may have peace. In the world you have tribulation, but take courage; I have overcome the world.

So, how do we get our minds around what Jesus is saying? First, and most important, keep all Scripture in context. While I do not include the passages that come before and after these verses, it is important to pay attention to what is said before and after each passage. Let me take it further. Be sure to keep each passage in the context of the entire book and each book in the context of the entire Bible from Genesis through Revelation. Yes, it takes time, but you need to know what in the *world* is going on!

Go, read the manual. In the meantime, I'll try to set up each verse for you, so it remains in context.

● Read the insight box concerning **tribulation**.

Here is where my mind goes: Jesus, I have questions. It just doesn't seem fair that in this *world* we will have "troubles, affliction, will be crushed, pressed, compressed, squeezed, and broken." Jesus can turn water into wine, heal the sick, and even raise the dead to life. Why can't Jesus make all the troubles go away?

God, why troubles?
If you are God, why not fix it?
If you are a good God, why don't you do something?
Why does it have to be like this?

If I've left any of your questions out, please add them. These are good questions that need answers. But how do we even start or go about finding answers to these questions in God's word?

Because you need to know how to discover God's Word for yourself, here are some tips:

Tip 1: A great tool for a topical Bible study like this one we are doing on *world* is biblegateway.com. There you can search the Bible for words like the *world, earth, ruler,* etc. Search for phrases like "ruler of this *world*" or "evil one" by putting quotes at either end of the phrase. When you search, it will pull up all the passages in the Bible that have the word or phrase that you entered. Then, read the passages to see what else God says in His Word on these

---

Tribulation (Thlipseos 2347) in the original language means… trouble, affliction, to crush, press, compress, squeeze, to break.

Zodhiates, Spiros: *The Complete Word Study Dictionary: New Testament*, electronic ed. Chattanooga, TN:AMG Publishers, ©1992, 1993, 2000, Strongs G2347

subjects and how they relate to each other. In addition to reading the passages, read what comes before and after. You might need to read an entire chapter or two or the whole book like I did with John.

Tip 2: As you read (1) mark in a distinctive way the word(s) or phrase(s) that started you on your search and (2) make a simple list of what you learn about each word or phrase.

Tip 3: You will also have the option to choose a variety of translations. You might want to start with the New American Standard. You can learn more about Bible translations from the American Bible Society[1].

Tip 4: Just find a translation that allows you to focus on getting to know God's character on a personal level and gain greater insight into His relationships with people.

Back to the main question. "Why can't Jesus make all the troubles go away?"

Let's start by looking at who is the ruler of this *world*? Let's look together to see what God's Word tells us about this *world*, the ruler of this *world*, and what these tell us about our lives in the *world*. As we do, please remember these aren't just words on a page, but God through His Word talking to you and me!

To help us find the answers to the questions, let's mark in a special way references to the *serpent*. So grab your pen or pencil, and as you read the following passage, when you see the word *serpent*, draw a pitchfork through the word.

Draw a pitchfork through *serpent*.

Read Genesis 3:1

> *Now the serpent was more crafty than any beast of the field which the LORD God had made. And he said to the woman, "Indeed, has God said, 'You shall not eat from any tree of the garden'?"*

- Look for your pitchfork. How is the serpent described?

Next, we'll discover the serpent has other names. Let's keep reading and looking so you can see for yourself. Continue to mark in a special way references to the *serpent*. Also, when you see the words *dragon*, *devil*, and *Satan*, draw a pitchfork through those words. Finally, watch for references to the *world*. When you see them, draw a circle around each reference to the *world*. Hang in there and just try, I promise, you will be amazed at what you discover for yourself.

Draw a pitchfork through references to *dragon*, *serpent*, *devil*, *Satan*.

Draw a circle around references to *world* or *earth*.

Read Revelation 12:7-9

⁷And there was war in heaven, Michael and his angels waging war with the dragon. The dragon and his angels waged war, ⁸and they were not strong enough, and there was no longer a place found for them in heaven. ⁹And the great dragon was thrown down, the serpent of old who is called the devil and Satan, who deceives the whole world; he was thrown down to the earth, and his angels were thrown down with him.

- Looking at the pitchforks, write out below all the names for the serpent.

- According to 7(b)-9, who waged war in heaven and what happened as a result?

- Look for your circle around the word *world*. What does the serpent do concerning the whole *world*?

- The word of God tells us that Satan came down to deceive the whole *world*. How does deception make for a wild ride and a crazy *world*? Explain to yourself below:

CHAPTER 3: IT'S A CRAZY WORLD!

- Are you part of the whole *world*? If so, should you consider yourself among the deceived?

- If deceived, how are you going to know it?

- On a scale of 1 (0% certainty) to 10 (100% certainty), how certain are you that you are telling yourself the truth about yourself, others, the *world,* God, and His Word?

    1   2   3   4   5   6   7   8   9   10

- How do the verses we have read and marked help you understand who the serpent was as described in Genesis 3:1 (page 43) and what he was doing to Eve? Explain below:

Let's keep reading, marking, and learning. As you read, mark *devil* with a pitchfork as well as synonyms like *he* and *him*. Also, watch for and mark any new names given to the *devil* with a pitchfork.

Draw a **pitchfork** through references to **devil** including pronouns like **he, him** or synonyms like **father, murderer, father of lies.**

Read John 8:44 (Jesus speaking to those who were seeking to kill Him)

You are of your father the devil, and you want to do the desires of your father. He was a murderer from the beginning, and does not stand in the truth because there is no truth in him. Whenever he speaks a lie, he speaks from his own nature, for he is a liar and the father of lies.

- Look at your pitchforks. What do you learn about the devil? How is he described?

- How does Jesus describe the people, and what does He say they are doing?

- How does this verse explain and help you understand the events described in Genesis 3:1 (page 43) and Revelation 12:7-9 (page 44)?

- What impact do people in the *world* (those who do the desires of the devil—a murderer and liar) have?

- How does that impact your *world*?

CHAPTER 3: IT'S A CRAZY WORLD!

Let's keep reading and marking all the passages that follow and then answering questions. I'll tell you what words to mark in each passage of Scripture before each Scripture reference.

Draw a **pitchfork** through references to *devil*.

Read 1 Peter 5:8

Be of sober spirit, be on the alert. Your adversary, the devil, prowls around like a roaring lion, seeking someone to devour.

- How is the devil described and what does he do?

- What are people instructed to do?

- If you are in a mental fog of lies and deception, how sober or alert are you?

- How does this passage explain and help you understand the events described in Genesis 3:1 (page 43), Revelation 12:7 (page 44), or the description of the devil given in John 8:44 (page 46)?

- Do you believe 1 Peter 5:8 applies to you? Why or why not?

- According to God, the devil was thrown down and deceives the whole *world* which would include you and me. In what ways might have the deception of the devil impacted your self-talk and what you believe about yourself, others, the *world* in general, and God? Explain below:

You have been deceived

You might have chuckled the first time I asked you to draw a pitchfork through the word serpent. You might still be wondering why I asked you to draw a pitchfork. It slows you down and causes you to read with a purpose. Also, when you go back to dig out what the passage says by asking questions, the pitchfork (or any marking) helps you easily find the answers.

As you can see from the pitchfork, the ruler of this *world* is the devil. He is the serpent of old who waged war, was thrown down with his angels, and deceives the whole *world*. A murderer and a liar from the beginning, he showed up way back in the beautiful garden that God planted for Adam and Eve. Eve was deceived.

You have been deceived. That's what he does, and he has you exactly where he wants you—believing lies. No? Go back and look at the things you wrote down and checked at the end of Chapter 1 concerning your self-talk.

How do you know if those things you checked are absolutely true? What better way for your adversary to devour you than to have you believing lies?

The struggle is real.

The scheme to deceive and destroy worked with Eve, and it works with us because the devil is a liar and the father of lies. Eve's scenario—she was deceived. She distorted God's Word. She saw that the fruit was pleasing to her and thought God was holding out on her, so she did what she thought was right in her own eyes.

- Does Eve's scenario match yours? If so, in what ways?

Sin entered the *world*

Before Jesus leaves this *world*, He wants those closest to Him to know and understand and remember certain things about the *world*. God, in His Word, has important things He wants us to know and understand and remember about this *world*. It's a need to know out of love and concern because there is a devil.

The devil is our adversary who deceives and continues to prowl. He seeks to destroy us just as he did Eve. We will fall into the same deception trap as Eve. God wants us to understand that what in

CHAPTER 3: IT'S A CRAZY WORLD!

the *world* happened on that day in the garden was that sin entered the *world*.

Getting our minds around sin and the impact sin had (and still has) on this *world* and on our lives personally is critical.

● How do you define sin and how did you arrive at that definition?

Now that you have had a chance to write down some thoughts regarding sin, let's go to God's Word to see what God says about sin. You know what to do. Read the passage, and as you read, mark the key words with the symbol listed above each Scripture referenced. Then, write out your answers to the questions that follow.

Circle every reference to **world**.

Draw a **box** around references to **sinned** and **sin**.

Read Romans 3:23

...for all have sinned and fall short of the glory of God.

Read Romans 5:12 (one man = Adam)

Therefore, just as through one man sin entered into the world, and death through sin, and so death spread to all men, because all sinned.

● How many have sinned and fall short of the glory of God?

● According to God's Word, what two things entered the *world* back in the beautiful garden?

● What two things spread and to how many did these two things spread?

● How many have sinned?

● According to God's Word, would you be included as someone who has sinned?

Draw a **box** around **sin**.

Read James 4:17

...to one who knows the right thing to do and does not do it, to him it is sin.

- According to God's Word, what is sin?

- Have you ever known the right thing to do and didn't do it?

Read Isaiah 53:6(a)

All of us like sheep have gone astray each of us has turned to his own way.

- How are you like sheep?

Draw a **box** around references to **sin**.

Draw a **circle** around references to **world**.

Read Ephesians 2:1-3 (Spoken to believers showing their condition before Christ, which is true of all people before Christ. More on this in the next chapter.)

¹And you were dead in your trespasses and sins, ²in which you formerly walked according to the course of this world, according to the prince of the power of the air, of the spirit that is now working in the sons of disobedience. ³Among them we too all formerly lived in the lusts of our flesh, indulging the desires of the flesh and of the mind, and were by nature children of wrath, even as the rest.

- Based on all of the Scriptures we have looked at about the ruler of this *world* the devil, who is the prince of the power of the air, the spirit that is now working in the sons of disobedience?

- According to verse 3, how do those who *"walk according to the course of this world, according to the prince of the power of the air"* behave?

CHAPTER 3: IT'S A CRAZY WORLD!

- According to verse 2, what or who is working in those who walk according to the *world*?

Satan + sinners = crazy *world*

Let's see if we can make a list that sums up the *world* and the people in the *world* based on what we've seen from God's Word. If you agree, check the box.

☐ The ruler of this *world* is Satan (devil, serpent of old, dragon) who waged war in heaven and was thrown down to earth with his angels (John 8:44;12:31, Revelation 12:7-9).
   ☐ Satan is a liar, a murderer, deceives the whole *world*—myself included (John 8:44, Revelation 12:7-9).
   ☐ Satan is my adversary who prowls, seeks to devour (2 Peter 5:8).

All men:
   ☐ Have sinned (Romans 3:23, Romans 5:12).
   ☐ Are dead in trespasses and sins.
   ☐ Walk according to the prince of the power of the air, live in the lusts of the flesh and indulge in the desire of the flesh and the mind (Ephesians 2:1-3).
   ☐ Do the desires of the devil (John 8:44, Ephesians 2:1-3).
   ☐ Do their own thing, turn their own way (Isaiah 53:6).

Are you telling yourself the truth?

The first time I went through Scripture reading and marking these same passages of Scripture and writing out answers, I was shocked. Who knew this about the *world*? No wonder I couldn't find my happily ever-after *world*. I started to wonder if I had been deceived on many levels. All these years later, I can tell you the answer to that question was a definite "Yes!"

> *No wonder I couldn't find my happily every-after world. I started to wonder if I had been deceived on many levels. All these years later, I can tell you the answer to that question was a definite "Yes!"*

51

SELF-TALK: Change your mind, change your life

Let me say it again. If you and I do not know the truth, or know where to find the truth, any old lie will do. As individuals, we are deceived because the whole *world* is deceived. The serpent of old was thrown down with his angels and deceives the whole *world*.

Lost and dazed in a fog of deception is exactly where the devil wants us—dead in our sins, walking according to his desire, and living according to our fleshly lusts. Going our own way and indulging in the desires both of flesh and mind.

The combination does not make for the happy life. Remember the *Inside Out* movie clip? Imagine that *Sadness* is crying buckets and *Fear* is flipping out when learning of this truth. The trouble that comes from living not only in a crazy *world* but going crazy has the emotional characters in your head running wild and your self-talk crazy.

Understanding from God's Word what is going on in the *world* around you, and why it is happening, will help you manage the way you view the *world* and what you tell yourself about the *world*. It will change your self-talk.

- Review what you wrote at the beginning of this chapter (page 39) about how you view the *world* and your life in it.

- How does what you believe about the *world*, the devil, and yourself line up with the Scriptures we've covered in this section? Write out how your self-talk lines up with God's Word, or does not line up with God's Word.

Life is a wild ride. Up, up, up you go and down, down, down you fly. Get a grip on the strong bar of God's Word and be prepared, because not only is it a wild ride, but it's a crazy *world*.

- Based on all the Scriptures we've covered in this chapter, explain to yourself why bad things happen in this *world*.

Take courage because there is more to the story, and it is beautiful!

Draw a **cross** through *Jesus* including pronouns.
Draw a **circle** around references to *world*.

Read John 16:33 (Jesus speaking)

These things I have spoken to you, so that in Me you may have peace. In the world you have tribulation, but take courage; I have overcome the world.

- Looking where you marked Jesus with a cross, answer the following questions:

  Where does Jesus say you may have peace?

  Why does Jesus say we are to take courage?

Yes! Bring on the peace, because this *world* is crazy. But what does it mean to find peace in Jesus in a crazy *world*? And how is it possible that Jesus has overcome the *world* when things are still so messed up? Good questions, because the answers impact what you and I think, what we believe, and how we live our lives. Let's keep digging.

#4 There's Good News

Jesus has overcome the *world*!

Up, up, up you go and down, down, down you fly on this wild ride of life. What you tell yourself during the ride shapes what you believe and how you behave. But, are you telling yourself the truth? Since you've been deceived, probably not. Satan + sinners = a crazy *world*. Help! But wait, didn't we end the last chapter discovering that Jesus has overcome the *world*?

This is a crazy, fallen *world* where the ruler of this *world* is the devil himself, the serpent of old. Well, no wonder Jesus said in this *world* we will have troubles. So surely overcoming the *world* means fixing it, overcoming all those troubles, and making it a perfect *world*, right?

No, that would be called heaven. But Jesus says to take courage because He has overcome the *world*. So what does that mean? Let's look at it together.

SELF-TALK: Change your mind, change your life

Read Philippians 2:6-9 (Amplified Bible)

*⁶...although **He (Jesus)** existed in the form and unchanging essence of God [as **One** with Him, possessing the fullness of all the divine attributes—the entire nature of deity], did not regard equality with God a thing to be grasped or asserted [as if **He** did not already possess it, or was afraid of losing it]; ⁷but emptied **Himself** [without renouncing or diminishing **His** deity, but only temporarily giving up the outward expression of divine equality and **His** rightful dignity] by assuming the form of a bond-servant, and being made in the likeness of men [**He** became completely human but was without sin, being fully God and fully man]. ⁸After **He** was found in [terms of **His**] outward appearance as a man [for a divinely-appointed time], **He** humbled **Himself** [still further] by becoming obedient [to the Father] to the point of death, even death on a cross. ⁹For this reason also [because **He** obeyed and so completely humbled **Himself**], God has highly exalted **Him** and bestowed on **Him** the name which is above every name.*

- According to verses 6-7, who is Jesus?

- Based on these verses, write out below what Jesus did. Look for where "**Himself, His, Him, He**" is in bold.

Jesus is fully God and fully man. How can it be? God's Word explains that Jesus became completely human, yet was without sin. Jesus emptied Himself. How? God left his throne in heaven and took on flesh, confined Himself to a human body, and humbled Himself to the point of death on a cross.

But why? As you read, draw a cross through references to Jesus. Let's see what we can discover.

CHAPTER 4: THERE'S GOOD NEWS

Draw a **cross** through references to **Jesus**.

Read Romans 6:23

For the wages of sin is death, but the free gift of God is eternal life in Christ Jesus our Lord.

- According to this verse:

  What is the wage or price or penalty for your sin?

  The free gift of God is eternal life in who?

- Read the insight box concerning **death**.

  What is death?

  What then is eternal life?

> **Death** (Thanatos 2288) in the original language means both physical death and exclusion from the presence and favor of God in consequence of sin and disobedience, but never as extinction. Spiritually speaking, we will live forever in either heaven with God or in hell, excluded from the presence and favor of God.
>
> Zodhiates, Spiros: *The Complete Word Study Dictionary: New Testament*, electronic ed. Chattanooga, TN:AMG Publishers, ©1992, 1993, and 2000, Strongs G2288

Remember that personal and intimate relationship that God had with Adam and Eve way back in the garden before the serpent of old entered the picture? Well, it is the same personal and intimate relationship God wants to have with each one of us. But, just like Adam and Eve, their disobedience, or sin, separated them from God. So too has our sin separated us from God.

The standard for a right relationship with God was set way back in that beautiful garden with Adam and Eve. Earlier we looked at Genesis 2:16-17 (see page 32), where God said that in the day they ate from the tree of the knowledge of good and evil they would surely die. The above definition concerning death applied to them just as it does to us.

They knew the right thing to do and didn't do it. They didn't do what God instructed them to do. They sinned.

As a result, Romans 5:12 tells us sin entered the *world*, and death through sin, so death spread to all men. A sad day for them as they went from intimacy with God to hiding from God. A sad day for us too.

Stop and think about the personal and intimate relationships you have. When you give someone full access to your heart and personal information, there are standards, promises or vows, and high trust levels involved. Let me remind you of what I said in Chapter 2 about the word standard. Standard means "something set up and established by authority as a rule for the measure of quantity, weight, extent, value, or quality."

When standards, promises or vows, and trust are broken, relationships are damaged and can be severed.

God, the Almighty, the Holy One, spoke the *world* into existence and the One who gives us life and breath, wants a personal and intimate relationship with you. He wants to give full access to His presence and promises, and wants you to know Him as personally as He knows you. It's amazing, really. It's only fitting, logical, and natural that in granting you all access, He would set clear standards for a right relationship with Him. Do you agree or disagree?

- Explain your answer below.

That day in the garden, rather than physically killing Adam and Eve, an animal was killed in their place. I don't know if you remember or not from our earlier reading, but Adam named each of the animals. How sobering it must have been to realize one of those animals he had named died in his place.

Read Genesis 3:2 (Amplified Bible)

The LORD God made tunics of [animal] skins for Adam and his wife and clothed them.

God made. Did you see that? In their disobedience and hiding, God approached them and made for them tunics of animal skins. How do I know an animal died that day?

Reason with me. Removing the skin of an animal would surely cause its death. Also, page after page in the Old Testament records God's standards for how His people were to sacrifice animals for the atonement of their sins, so they could continue to live and be in right relationship with Him.

In fact, God explains in Leviticus 17:11 that life is in the blood. The blood of an animal shed means the life of an animal was given

CHAPTER 4: THERE'S GOOD NEWS

in their place, so they might live and be in right relationship with Him. The debt for their sin was paid. An animal died in their place. God approached them. God provided for them so they could live and be in right relationship with Him. He loved them so much.

Guess what? He loves us like that too.

Read John 3:16

For God so loved the world, that He gave His only begotten Son, that whoever believes in Him shall not perish, but have eternal life.

For God so loved the *world* that He sent Jesus. God wants us to be in right relationship with Him, so He provided what was needed to satisfy the sin debt then and now so that we could have a relationship with Him. A relationship. Wow!

God knows we are helpless and unable to meet His standard. *"For all have sinned and fall short of the glory of God"* (Romans 3:23). That's why Jesus left His throne in heaven, emptied Himself, confined Himself to a human body, and humbled Himself to the point of death on a cross. Jesus provided for us a once-and-for-all payment for sin—a free gift. God approaches us. God provides for us so that we can live and be in right relationship with Him.

Let's look again at Romans 6:23 which says, *"For the wages of sin is death, but the free gift of God is eternal life in Christ Jesus our Lord."*

- Based on Romans 6:23, what excludes, or did exclude, you from the presence of God and from having the favor of God?

- Based on Romans 6:23, what free gift is God offering, and what does that free gift provide?

- Explain to yourself one more time what is eternal life.

Draw a **cross** through references to **Christ**.

Read Romans 5:6-8

> ⁶For while we were still helpless, at the right time Christ died for the ungodly. ⁷For one will hardly die for a righteous man; though perhaps for the good man someone would dare even to die. ⁸But God demonstrates His own love toward us, in that while we were yet sinners, Christ died for us.

- According to these verses, how are those for whom Christ died described?

- Based on verse 8, what was God demonstrating?

Ungodly and sinners who are helpless to do anything about it. Yep, that's us. But, there is good news for the *world*, and that good news is Jesus.

The helpless accept the help

There is a choice to be made. Stay dead in our sins, let the devil be our father, live in deception, indulge in the desires of our flesh and mind, and spend both now and eternity separated from God's presence and favor. Or, we can accept God's free gift of eternal life in Christ Jesus. We might protest, telling ourselves we are good people, and perhaps compared to others, we are good people. But according to God's Word in Romans 5:6-8, we are still dead in our sins. Please don't be deceived.

Read Hebrews 4:15-16 (The Message)

> ¹⁴⁻¹⁶Now that we know what we have—Jesus, this great High Priest with ready access to God—let's not let it slip through our fingers. We don't have a priest who is out of touch with our reality. He's been through weakness and testing, experienced it all—all but the sin. So, let's walk right up to him and get what he is so ready to give. Take the mercy, accept the help.

CHAPTER 4: THERE'S GOOD NEWS

Take the mercy. Accept the help.

Draw a **cross** through references to *Jesus*.

Read John 14:6

Jesus said to him, "I am the way, and the truth, and the life; no one comes to the Father but through Me."

- What four (4) things does Jesus tell you about Himself?

Draw a **cross** through references to *Jesus*.

Read 2 Corinthians 5:21

He (God) made Him (Jesus) who knew no sin to be sin on our behalf, so that we might become the righteousness of God in Him (Jesus).

Read 2 Corinthians 5:21 (The Message)

How? You ask. In Christ. God put the wrong on him, who never did anything wrong, so we could be put right with God.

- According to this passage, what did God make Jesus be?

- How is this good news for you and the *world*?

- Read the insight box concerning **righteousness**.

- According to this passage, what did God do so that you might become righteous before Him or made right with Him?

Righteousness
(Dikaiosune 1343) in the original language means those on whom God bestows His righteousness become righteous before God.

Zodhiates, Spiros: *The Complete Word Study Dictionary: New Testament*, electronic ed. Chattanooga, TN:AMG Publishers, ©1992, 1993, and 2000, Strongs G1343

SELF-TALK: Change your mind, change your life

Please stop now and watch a short video entitled: *Jesus on the Cross, A Medical Perspective*[1]. You can find the video in the resources section of my website at sallyhhall.com.

Jesus endured great suffering for you and me. His blood was shed for us. The death Jesus died was for us and in our place in order to pay our sin debt in full. He, who knew no sin, became sin on our behalf, yours and mine, so that we could be right with God and enjoy a personal and intimate relationship with God.

The heart cannot love what the mind does not know. –Jen Wilkin[2]

This quote by Jen Wilkin is so true! So as you read the following passages, ask the Lord to help you wrap your mind around them so your heart can love them. Take them personally and to heart!

Let's add some additional symbols as we read to see what we can discover about the blood and death of Jesus.

Draw a **cross** through references to **Jesus** or **Christ**.
Draw a **$** through **redemption** and **redeemed**.
Double-underline every reference to the **blood**.

Read Ephesians 1:7

In Him (Jesus) we have redemption through His blood, the forgiveness of our trespasses (sins), according to the riches of His grace.

Read 1 Peter 1:18-19

[18]knowing that you were not redeemed with perishable things like silver or gold from your futile way of life inherited from your forefathers, [19]but with precious blood, as of a lamb unblemished and spotless, the blood of Christ.

- Read the insight box concerning **redeemed** and **forgiveness**.

This is why a $ symbol is a good symbol to remind us that redemption costs something. In this case, the life and blood of Jesus.

- According to these verses, what does the blood of Jesus provide?

- How precious to you is the blood of Jesus? Take time now to write out your thoughts.

Redeemed (Lutroo 3084) in the original language means to bring forth a ransom; to release by receipt of a ransom. In other words, there is a cost involved that must be paid in order for there to be a release.

Zodhiates, Spiros: *The Complete Word Study Dictionary: New Testament*, electronic ed. Chattanooga, TN:AMG Publishers, ©1992, 1993, and 2000, Strongs G3084

Forgiveness in the original language means (1) a release from bondage or imprisonment and (2) a forgiveness or pardon of sins. Letting them go as if they had never been committed and a remission of the penalty.

Thayer and Smith. Greek Lexicon entry for Peripateo. The NAS New Testament Greek Lexicon 1999

CHAPTER 4: THERE'S GOOD NEWS

Draw a **cross** through references to **Jesus**.
Double-underline references to **blood**.

Read Romans 5:9-10 (Amplified Bible)

⁹Therefore, since we have now been justified [declared free of the guilt of sin] by His blood, [how much more certain is it that] we will be saved from the wrath of God through Him. ¹⁰For if while we were enemies we were reconciled to God through the death of His Son, it is much more certain, having been reconciled, that we will be saved [from the consequences of sin] by His life [that is, we will be saved because Christ lives today].

- Before being justified and saved, what does verse 10 say about your relationship to God and what was or is upon you?

- Based on all you have read, what would the wrath of God be?

- Read the insight box concerning **justified**.
- According to verse 9, what two things do you learn that the blood and death of Jesus provide?

- Read the insight box concerning **reconciled**.

God has gone even further than paying the penalty for our sin, and allowed us to escape judgment and His wrath. By Jesus' death, we have also become friends with God. We are no longer enemies but reconciled with God. To this my soul says "wow!"

- According to verse 10, what did the death of Jesus provide?

Justified (Dikaioo 1344) in the original language means declared right with God. It is a legal term that indicates the payment for a sin penalty has been fully paid. To be justified means the penalty for your sin has been totally paid and in the eyes of God you stand not guilty.

Zodhiates, Spiros: *The Complete Word Study Dictionary: New Testament*, electronic ed. Chattanooga, TN:AMG Publishers, ©1992, 1993, and 2000, Strongs G1344

Reconciled (Katallasso 2644) in the original language means to change. To reconcile. Used of the divine work of redemption denoting that act of redemption insofar as God Himself is concerned by taking upon Himself our sin and becoming an atonement. Thus a relationship of peace with mankind is established. In the NT, spoken of the change that God makes in man through conversion so that he may be reconciled to the holy God.

Zodhiates, Spiros: *The Complete Word Study Dictionary: New Testament*, electronic ed. Chattanooga, TN: AMG Publishers, ©1992, 1993, and 2000, Strongs G2644

We are redeemed with the precious blood of Jesus. When you and I were at our absolute worst—ungodly, sinners, and helpless to do anything about it—that is when God demonstrated His great love toward us. Jesus came to die in our place. It's good news that changes everything for us.

It breaks my heart to think of all the harm that living in this crazy *world* might have brought and still can bring you. The list includes harmful, hurtful, and destructive words and relationships; people whose father is, let's face it—the devil; and people who indulge in the devil's desires to destroy you.

Tears well up in my eyes thinking of you being abused, neglected, abandoned, rejected, robbed of your innocence, deceived, confused, and more. Yes, I want to start snatching people bald headed[3], but more so, I want to cup your face in my hands, lock eyes with you, and plead with you to listen to me. There's good news for you, and there is good news for the *world*. I cannot change the reality of what has happened to you but there is good news. The good news is Jesus. He came to redeem you and purchase you with His very own blood. Your life has great value, meaning, and purpose to Him. So much so that he left heaven for you and died for you so you could live now and forever in relationship with Him.

Look to the cross and Jesus' last words spoken on that cross.

Read John 19:30

Therefore, when Jesus had received the sour wine, He said, "It is finished!" And He bowed His head and gave up His spirit.

Right before Jesus died, he cried out "it is finished" which can also be translated "paid in full". Three words in English, but one word in Greek: **tetelestai**. In those days, when a debt had been paid in full, the word *tetelestai* was stamped or written across the certificate of debt and nailed where all could see. The last words spoken by Jesus were to you, saying I have paid your sin debt in full—it is finished!

- According to verse 30, combined with the information in the previous paragraph, write out below what was Jesus saying to you right before He died.

CHAPTER 4: THERE'S GOOD NEWS

How did Jesus overcome the *world*? Jesus, having died to sin once and for all, canceled out our certificate of debt. Jesus satisfied and paid the penalty for sin, which is death. Death could not hold Jesus. The below verses explain this much better than I can.

Read Hebrews 2:14-15

Therefore, since the children share in flesh and blood, He Himself (Jesus) likewise also partook of the same, that through death He (Jesus) might render powerless him who had the power of death, that is, the devil.

- According to this verse:

  Who had the power of death?

  How did Jesus render the devil powerless?

Read Acts 2: 24

²⁴But God raised Him (Jesus) up again, putting an end to the agony of death, since it was impossible for Him (Jesus) to be held in its power.

- Based on all we've discovered, what would be the agony of death?

- According to this verse, how did Jesus put an end to this agony?

Accept the gift

We each have a choice to make. Stay dead in sin or accept God's free gift of eternal life in Christ Jesus. Let's keep reading, marking, and discovering. Remember, the marking helps us to slow down, read with a purpose, and answer the questions that will follow.

Draw a **cross** through references to ***Jesus***.
Draw a **heart** through references to ***believe(s)***.
Draw an **oval** a big zero through references to ***confess(es)***.

Read Romans 10:9-10

⁹that if you confess with your mouth Jesus as Lord, and believe in your heart that God raised Him from the dead, you will be saved; ¹⁰for with the heart a person believes, resulting in righteousness, and with the mouth he confesses, resulting in salvation.

- Based on all the passages of Scripture covered in the chapters of this book so far, why is your salvation needed and important?

Lord (Kurios 2962) in the original language means owner, master. As possessor, owner, master of something and having absolute authority over.

Zodhiates, Spiros: *The Complete Word Study Dictionary: New Testament*, electronic ed. Chattanooga, TN: AMG Publishers, ©1992, 1993, and 2000, Strongs G2962

- Read the insight box concerning **Lord**.

- According to verse 9:

  What are you to confess with your mouth?

  What are you to believe in your heart?

  What is the result of confessing with your mouth Jesus as Lord and believing in your heart that God raised Jesus from the dead?

- According to verse 10:

  What is the result of believing in the heart?

  What is the result of confessing with the mouth?

  Do you need or want to be saved and declared right with God?

- Based on all the passages we've looked at in this chapter, from what are you saved?

Draw a **heart** through ***believe***.

Read James 2:19

You believe that God is one. You do well; the demons also believe, and shudder.

- What do you learn about demons?

The demons are those angels that were thrown down to earth with the devil way back when. The demons believe. They believe so much that they are moved to emotion. They shudder. It's interesting and odd to me that we can have this in common with the demons. We can believe all we read and hear concerning Jesus, and sometimes it can move us to the point of deep emotion, but it doesn't change our minds or the direction of our lives. Believing and confessing is much more than accepting a fact.

Your confession declares you acknowledge that only Christ can save you from the penalty of your sins, which is eternal separation from the presence and favor of God. You confess you are trusting in the death of Jesus alone to justify you and bring you into fellowship or peace with God. Therefore, in declaring Him as Lord, you place your life and all your hope in Him. Believing in your heart that God raised Jesus from the dead is complete confidence and trust that Jesus alone paid for and satisfied your sin debt, defeating the power of sin and death over your life. It means trusting in God's power and love which transforms your mind and life. You trust His promises of life, hope, righteousness, and peace.

This belief is very different from what the demons believe.

- Have you ever confessed with your mouth Jesus as owner and master, who possesses absolute authority over your life? Have you believed in your heart that God raised Him from the dead? If not, why not? Explain below.

To confess Jesus as Lord means you submit to the authority of God's Word and will over your life. No longer devoid of truth, you start living by the truth. You will live your life based on how God's Word says you should live because you trust Him and have put all of your trust in Him. Your self-talk becomes God-talk. More and more, you think, act, and behave according to the truth rather than according to the *world*. God's Word and your personal and intimate relationship with Jesus impact your mind and life, and power your ride.

Also, because of Jesus, your life here in this crazy *world* takes on new purpose and meaning. We'll explore this more together in the chapters to come. But for now, let me close out this chapter by asking you a very important question.

- How would you describe your **relationship** with Jesus?

    ☐ I am intimate with Jesus my Lord. (Jesus has absolute authority over my life. With the absolute authority of God's Word applied to my life, how I view myself, others, circumstances, and the *world* around me has changed. It is a priority relationship.)

    ☐ I am acquainted with and believe in Jesus. (I believe in Jesus. I am moved to attend or have attended Bible studies. I listen to sermons and sometimes discover and personally experience truth in a way that comforts and convicts me. I have experienced personal transformation from time to time. I do not surrender total authority to Jesus making Him Lord. I keep control. It is not a priority relationship.)

    ☐ I am distant from and not interested in getting to know Jesus intimately. (I hear the Word of God, and sometimes am moved by the Word of God but not in a way that changes my life or moves me to desire to become better acquainted, develop an intimate relationship, or make a priority relationship.)

CHAPTER 4: THERE'S GOOD NEWS

Beginning in the next chapter, I will be talking to you as one who has confessed Jesus as Lord, and who is pursuing a personal and intimate relationship with Him. It is important for me to make this distinction clear to you, because my intimate relationship with Jesus and your intimate relationship (see description on page 68) with Jesus gives us access to God. People only acquainted with or distant from Jesus cannot and do not have this access. Remember John 14:6 where Jesus says, *"I am the way, and the truth, and the life; no one comes to the Father but through Me."*

If you still aren't sure about your relationship with Jesus, keep reading, digging and discovering. Just remember, those in an intimate relationship with Jesus have been declared right with God, have been forgiven of sins, have eternal life, and so much more. These truths in the middle of a crazy *world* change our thinking about ourselves and the *world* around us. These truths significantly impact our **self-talk**.

Knowing these truths will mentally and emotionally prepare you for and help you manage the wild ride of life in a crazy *world*! Change your mind, change your life!

#5 You Are a Masterpiece

Created in Christ Jesus for good works—in the *world*

Read Ephesians 2:10

For we are His (God's) workmanship, created in Christ Jesus for good works, which God prepared beforehand so that we would walk in them.

The New Living Translations says: *"For we are God's masterpiece…".*

- Based on Ephesians 2:10, whose workmanship or masterpiece are you?

- In whom have you been created?

- Why have you been created in Christ Jesus?

- Read the insight box concerning **good works** and **walk**.

- According to verse 10, when were good works prepared for you?

- What are you to do concerning these good works?

This is a lot of truth to get your mind around, yet this truth is key to mentally and emotionally preparing for and managing the wild ride of life in a crazy *world*!

Good works (Ergon 2041) in the original language means work, i.e., deed, act, action, something done. Of good works, benevolent work, or good deeds.

Zodhiates, Spiros: *The Complete Word Study Dictionary: New Testament*, electronic ed. Chattanooga, TN: AMG Publishers, ©1992, 1993, and 2000, Strongs G2041

Walk (Peripateo 4043) in the original language means to walk; to make one's way, progress; to make due use of opportunities. To live (1) to regulate one's life (2) to conduct one's self (3) to pass one's life.

Thayer and Smith. Greek Lexicon entry for Peripateo. The NAS New Testament

Grasping mentally and emotionally the truth that you are God's masterpiece gives you the confidence you need to walk in the good works prepared just for you. You are uniquely you for a very good purpose! This verse is now part of your self-talk.

> **Being created in Christ Jesus is your new beginning. Next, you'll learn to see yourself and the world around you through the eyes of God via His Word—truth. The truth will reveal and dispel the lies you have been believing.**

Remember, from this point on in the book, I am talking to you as one who is pursuing a personal and intimate relationship with Jesus as Lord.

Being created in Christ Jesus is your new beginning. Next, you'll learn to see yourself and the *world* around you through the eyes of God via His word—truth. The truth will reveal and dispel the lies you have been believing.

Let's not forget, Satan deceives the whole *world*. You and I formerly walked according to the *world* and were ourselves deceived (Ephesians 2:1-3). Whether you confessed Jesus as Lord and believed in your heart God raised Him from the dead years ago or yesterday, your mind has a mix of messages that must constantly be filtered and measured against the truth of God's Word to ensure that you do not believe lies. Being mentally tangled in a web of lies is exactly where your adversary wants you. He does not want you to know or realize that Jesus rendered him powerless. Every day new messages and experiences flood your mind. You can still be deceived. But now, praise God, you are no longer devoid of truth.

No longer devoid of truth, you now can recognize, think, and walk in truth. You understand God has a plan and a purpose for your life, right here, right now, and in this crazy *world*. Truth tells you that before He spoke the *world* into existence, He thought of you, planned for you, and prepared good works, deeds, acts, and actions just for you. Because you do not want to miss what God has planned for you, you must retrain your mind to think and talk to yourself based on what God says in His Word. Your thoughts cannot be based on what you've always thought or felt and said to yourself in the past. Created in Christ Jesus, this is the new you!

On a scale of 1 (0%) to 10 (100%):

- How confident are you that you truly are God's masterpiece?

    1   2   3   4   5   6   7   8   9   10

- Do you possess the confidence needed to walk in the good works prepared beforehand for you, no matter what obstacles come your way?

    1   2   3   4   5   6   7   8   9   10

- Are you mentally prepared to walk in the good works prepared beforehand for you? Meaning, are you mentally prepared to accomplish and complete the work God has prepared for you no matter what comes at you?

    1   2   3   4   5   6   7   8   9   10

Let's be honest. Most of us start at #1 (0%), but taking the time to assess our confidence and preparedness levels ensures we keep growing and are better prepared.

We recently enjoyed a four-day visit with family. As we spent time getting caught up, our niece, who has a Master's Degree in Sports Psychology, shared about her work as a volunteer with the local Miss America organization. Through her involvement, she realized the organization was not focused on beauty, but rather on investing in the lives of young women who could bring social change through education and service. Her favorite part has been coaching young women who compete in the pageants. Part of their coaching is called "mental management."

Fascinated, I asked my niece more questions. She used the example of the poise and confidence needed during each segment of the competition. They have one opportunity during each segment (swimsuit, talent, gown, interview) to shine with poise and confidence and outshine the others because, of course, there is the panel of judges. No pressure, right? But coaches mentally prepare each contestant based on individual strengths, weaknesses, and potential scenarios.

My niece and I talked briefly about the mental confidence needed, especially for the swimsuit competition, and the value of having a coach to help you mentally prepare for "that" moment. This concept of mental management is brilliant, and it preaches!

I've been part of churches and organizations that did mentoring, disciplining, coaching, and some included role playing, but nothing that went to this level of mental management. Why don't we do more mental coaching? Imagine being mentally and emotionally prepared ahead of time for real life, real *world*, and everyday situations. As I sat listening to my niece, I wondered if perhaps the name of this book should be Mental Management.

Let me be clear. I am not saying that in life we "psych" ourselves out or up. I am not suggesting that we tell ourselves or have coaches that tell us "whatever" so that we feel better about ourselves or our circumstances. That could be like saying any old lie will do or leaving it up to *Joy, Sadness, Fear, Anger,* and *Disgust*, etc. to decide what to do based on what "feels right." Psyching ourselves out or up, based on what we think is or "feels right," is not the answer.

I am declaring it is a huge relief to know that in every situation, we can and should take up the manual of God's Word. Every situation has a truth filter. Also, God sends people into our lives who can and should take up His Word and coach us by speaking truth into each situation. Either way, truth (God's Word) coaches us, and as a result, we can be mentally and emotionally prepared for every situation.

So, why don't we see more of this kind of real life, real *world*, everyday situation, mental management coaching using the Word of God? It's baffling, and my only answer is that we must not know that everything about life and living life is in this manual. Deception abounds.

Here is a truth about you. Before God spoke the *world* into existence, He thought of you, planned for you, prepared good works for you, and preserved His Word which shows you how to accomplish the good work.

- How does this truth change your mind or thinking?

- If your mind knows this truth about you and your heart loves it, how has or will it change your life?

You are God's masterpiece

The first step in being mentally and emotionally prepared to walk into the work God has prepared, is getting your mind fully wrapped around the truth that you are God's masterpiece created in Christ Jesus. Only then will you gain the confidence and knowledge needed to walk out into the crazy *world* and accomplish the good works that God planned for you beforehand, or before He spoke the *world* into existence.

Knowing and understanding the truths from God's Word about who you are as His adopted child, what is yours in Christ, and how to walk and talk in the *world* will give you the confidence you need to be mentally and emotionally prepared for every situation.

Let me give you an example. Remember the Miss America swimsuit competition I mentioned? The mention of swimsuit causes alarms to go off in my head. As in the movie *Inside Out*, that's control center in the hands of *Fear* and *Disgust*, and it is a wild and crazy scene. Parading myself in front of the *world* in a swimsuit is the worst kind of pageantry. The looks and sneers of the unknown judges can be harsh and severe. (You probably want to start coaching me right now, don't you? Good for you!) Mentally and emotionally, it's easier to avoid the swimsuit, which means avoiding the pool, beach, and all water activity. Is anyone with me here? Yes, avoidance solves that problem.

But wait! Avoidance means missing out on time with family and friends who are going to be doing these things without me. I miss opportunities to love on, share Jesus, and pray for or with others. I miss potential "good works." Come on, I miss having fun! But, here's what I have learned. I learned that the truth about who I am in Christ allows me to mentally and emotionally manage my fear and anxiety, and gives me the courage to walk out the door.

Read Romans 9:25

> *I will call those who were not My people, "My people." And her who was not beloved, "beloved."*

The word beloved means to esteem, love, indicating a direction of the will and finding one's joy in something or someone.

You are Beloved of God

This truth takes my breath away every time I read it. As children of God, when there was nothing beloved about you and me, that's when God declared us beloved. Being esteemed by God is no small thing. This truth gives courage. Knowing that God, the Creator, takes joy in me makes my emotional character *Joy* jump! How about you?

Retraining my mind to remember and recall this truth helps me mentally manage my old emotions and default self-talk of "you don't measure up" and "rejection." As I walk out the door in my black and white polka dot swim dress, pink flip flops and pink float, and head to the water with my family and friends, I remind myself I am beloved of God. I measure up to God. He has not and will never reject me. God finds joy in me. He has things He wants me to do on His behalf with and for my family and friends. I am loved by God—the one who spoke the *world* into existence, keeps the *world* hanging in the middle of nothing, who gives life and breath, and sent Jesus to die in my place. I am secure in Jesus.

Sure, walking out the door in that swim dress get-up is still a risk. It takes courage. I can still be rejected and feel like I don't measure up. The *world* isn't going to see me the same way God sees me, but grasping the truth that I am His masterpiece and His beloved gives me the courage I need. I can also show the *world* Jesus and have confidence to walk out into the *world*, do the work prepared for me, and have joy in doing it!

Whatever your "swimsuit" scenarios are, you must prepare your mind ahead of time, so you have the courage and confidence needed to walk out into this crazy *world* and do the work prepared for you. If you are not mentally and emotionally prepared, you can miss the work prepared for you. You do not want to do that. You really don't. Remember, you have an adversary who is doing everything possible to try to keep you from knowing this truth and living in the light of this truth.

Retrain your mind

The kind of self-talk that devalues, demoralizes, demeans, and robs you of your self confidence, is the kind of self-talk that keeps you from reaching your full potential in Christ and must be hushed. Everything you once thought and every message from those around you and what the *world* once told you, is still stored in that mind of yours. Have you been telling yourself the truth?

Thinking and self-talk that does not line up with God's Word must first be identified. Self-talk that doesn't line up with God's Word is a lie. Remember, all of God's Word is absolute truth. Will you decide to pick and choose from God's Word what is true or not? Or, will you stand on all of God's Word as absolute truth?

Here's an exercise. Go back and review the negative body image section in Chapter 1 (page 21) where you wrote down a few of the things you think, believe, or have been told about the way you look.

Now, let's consider what God says about you.

In all the passages that follow in this chapter, **draw** a **triangle** through references to ***God***.

Read Psalm 139:1-18

¹O LORD, You have searched me and known me. ²You know when I sit down and when I rise up; You understand my thought from afar. ³You scrutinize my path and my lying down, And are intimately acquainted with all my ways. ⁴Even before there is a word on my tongue, Behold, O LORD, You know it all. ⁵You have enclosed me behind and before, And laid Your hand upon me. ⁶Such knowledge is too wonderful for me; It is too high, I cannot attain to it. ⁷Where can I go from Your Spirit? Or where can I flee from Your presence? ⁸If I ascend to heaven, You are there; If I make my bed in Sheol, behold, You are there. ⁹If I take the wings of the dawn, If I dwell in the remotest part of the sea, ¹⁰Even there Your hand will lead me, And Your right hand will lay hold of me. ¹¹If I say, "Surely the darkness will overwhelm me, And the light around me will be night," ¹²Even the darkness is not dark to You, And the night is as bright as the day. Darkness and light are alike to You. ¹³For You formed my inward parts; You wove me in my mother's womb. ¹⁴I will give thanks to You, for I am fearfully and wonderfully made; Wonderful are Your works, And my soul knows it very well. ¹⁵My frame was not hidden from You, When I was made in secret, And skillfully wrought in the depths of the earth; ¹⁶Your eyes have seen my unformed substance; And in Your book were all written The days that were ordained for me, When as yet there was not one of them. ¹⁷How precious also are Your thoughts to me, O God! How vast is the sum of them! ¹⁸If I should count them, they would outnumber the sand. When I awake, I am still with You.

- Starting at verse 1, list all the ways God knows you and things He knows about you:

- Does anyone know you as personally and intimately as God?

- According to verses 17-18, how are God's thoughts towards you described and how many are there?

CHAPTER 5: YOU ARE A MASTERPIECE

- Get a picture in your mind of all the sand on all the beaches and in all the deserts around the *world*. Do you realize that God's precious thoughts toward you outnumber the sand?

From a looks standpoint, I'd always been aware and told that I favor my father and his side of the family. Some parts of that I liked and others not so much. In the last years of my parent's lives, we had the privilege of caring for them and having them live with us.

When I would take my father to doctor appointments, I began to realize just how like him I was. On our first trip together to a podiatrist, I almost fell out of my chair when I realized I have my father's feet. I mean, if you put our feet in a lineup they would be twins. These are not the feet I would have picked for myself.

Scheduling our annual dermatologist visits at the same time seemed like a good use of time. My father would be in one room and me in the adjoining room. During one visit, and after examining my father, the doctor came in to let me know what was going on with my father and to give me my exam. I was asking about some new spots that had appeared on my body, and her explanation for this was, "Look at your father. It's genetics." Evidently, I come from a spotted people. Psalm 139 moves me to see my feet, my spots, and everything about myself through the eyes of God. I am reminded I am fearfully and wonderfully made.

Maybe you have determined or been told that your forehead or nose is too big. Maybe you want different feet. You could send off for the Ancestry DNA testing, but the one who determined my feet and spots is the same One who determined your DNA before He ever spoke the *world* into existence. He determined and knew your ancestors (family) before there was yet any one of them. He planned for you and declared that you are fearfully and wonderfully made. What about deformities and defects? I don't know. What does God say? Maybe we just need to understand that God sees things very differently than we see things. Maybe our fog of deception and thinking as the *world* thinks has kept us from seeing and understanding the truth about our looks, our lives, and the One who created us.

- According to Psalm139:1-18, who determined everything about you?

- In what ways does your body image match God's image of you?

- Does God say anything that addresses any specific insecurities you have? If so, list the insecurities and His word that specifically addresses them.

- Based on what God says about you (God-talk), write down your self-talk that needs to change and needs to stop.

- Write below how Psalm 139:1-18 mentally coaches you or helps you manage your self-talk, so that you have the confidence needed to walk in the good works prepared for you. What's the God-talk?

Every time I read this Psalm 139:13, I picture God sitting on His throne in the heavens, weaving or knitting us together. Hands on, tenderly forming us, creating us, anticipating us, and planning our days for us. No matter what I feel, think, or what others tell me, my life has meaning and purpose because God Himself planned for and created me, knows me intimately, and He thinks of me.

He chose the color of my skin, hair, eyes, and shaped my nose, ears, hands, feet, toes, body shape—all of it. He knitted me together. He designed each birthmark, genetic strand, imperfection, and irregularity. He has declared I am fearfully and wonderfully made. He knows what I am going to say even before I say it. He knows everything about me, and I am never out of His sight. You can bet that when I am on the beach, Psalm 139:17-18 strengthens me. I can silence the *world* because I saw in the manual of God's Word,

CHAPTER 5: YOU ARE A MASTERPIECE

with my very own eyes, that I can look to the sand and remember His precious thoughts toward me outnumber that sand. This causes me to shift my feelings of "rejection" and "not measuring up" to God's precious thoughts toward me.

There are nerve-wracking, frightening, vulnerable, "trigger" moments when our self-talk is ruled by *Joy, Fear, Anger, Disgust, Sadness, Shame,* etc. It's a given that life's wild ride in a crazy *world* will send our emotions running around crazy in our heads. In those moments, you won't feel like a masterpiece or beloved of God. What others have told you and what you've told yourself will be your default thinking.

The things you might have written down or checked off in chapter 1 (*I am unloved, ugly, all alone, unwanted, no one cares, etc.*) are examples of default thinking. Learning and choosing to allow what God says in His Word to rule over all the ugly, harmful, hurtful, painful, horrible truths in your life is the key to reaching your full potential in Christ. Learning to mentally and emotionally manage using God's Word is key. Remember, as you allow God's Word to wash over you, your self-talk, now God-talk will give you courage and confidence to walk out and in the good works prepared for you beforehand. Truth can and will change the way you think and walk. Change your mind, change your life!

Read Psalm 56:8

You have taken account of my wanderings; Put my tears in Your bottle. Are they not in Your book?

How precious is it that God cares so much for you that He collects your tears in a bottle? Well okay, maybe there is a room full of bottles, or two or three rooms, or a heavenly warehouse, but let's not get hung up on technicalities. Let's stick to the point. God cares deeply and intimately about you. Remember, we live in a *world* that brings suffering. In this *world*, there are lots and lots of troubles. We'll talk more about troubles in a later chapter. We will have troubles and sometimes those troubles send us wandering. But, we are never alone, and we are never out of His sight or thoughts, even when wandering and weeping. He sees, He knows, and He cares.

- Describe how this verse mentally coaches you or helps you manage your self-talk. How does this truth give you the confidence needed to walk in the good works prepared for you?

Read Romans 8:31-35, 37-39

³¹What then shall we say to these things? If God is for us, who is against us? ³²He who did not spare His own Son, but delivered Him over for us all, how will He not also with Him freely give us all things? ³³Who will bring a charge against God's elect? God is the one who justifies; ³⁴who is the one who condemns? Christ Jesus is He who died, yes, rather who was raised, who is at the right hand of God, who also intercedes for us. ³⁵Who will separate us from the love of Christ? Will tribulation, or distress, or persecution, or famine, or nakedness, or peril, or sword?

³⁷But in all these things we overwhelmingly conquer through Him who loved us. ³⁸For I am convinced that neither death, nor life, nor angels, nor principalities, nor things present, nor things to come, nor powers, ³⁹nor height, nor depth, nor any other created thing, will be able to separate us from the love of God, which is in Christ Jesus our Lord.

- Based on verse 31, who is for you?

- Based on verse 32,
  Has God or will God ever hold out on you?

  What will God freely give to you?

- According to verse 34, who intercedes or prays for you?

- Based on verses 35-39, what can separate you from the love of God in Christ Jesus?

- What do you learn from verse 37?

CHAPTER 5: YOU ARE A MASTERPIECE

- According to verses 35-39 what do you overwhelmingly conquer and how?

The truth is, God is for you, and He loves you. No matter how wild the ride gets, or crazy the *world* is, you overwhelmingly conquer through Him, and nothing or no one can or will ever separate you from the love of God in Jesus. Coach yourself using these truths and they will change the way you think, feel, and live.

- Describe how these verses mentally coach you or help you manage your self-talk. How do these truths give you the confidence needed to walk in the good works prepared for you?

SELF-TALK: Change your mind, change your life

Read Isaiah 43:1–4, 25

¹But now, thus says the Lord, your Creator, O Jacob, And He who formed you, O Israel, "Do not fear, for I have redeemed you; I have called you by name; you are Mine! ²"When you pass through the waters, I will be with you; And through the rivers, they will not overflow you. When you walk through the fire, you will not be scorched, nor will the flame burn you. ³For I am the Lord your God, The Holy One of Israel, your Savior; I have given Egypt as your ransom, Cush and Seba in your place. ⁴Since you are precious in My sight, since you are honored and I love you, I will give other men in your place and other peoples in exchange for your life."

²⁵I, even I, am the one who wipes out your transgressions for My own sake, And I will not remember your sins."

- While these words were to the nation of Israel, in what ways has God spoken the message and the words through Jesus?

Stop and ponder the truths of these verses realized in Jesus. God formed you, redeemed you with the blood of Jesus, calls you by name, and says "you are Mine." Surely your mind went to those little multicolored Valentine candy hearts. 100% sugar. If there were a candy heart from God, it would say "You are Mine" rather than "Be Mine." The One who formed you goes on to say—I am with you, you are precious and honored, and I love you. 100% sweet.

I am no medical doctor, psychologist, or scientist, but I can tell you from personal experience that when humans are in a relationship where they are loved, honored, esteemed, and valued like this, they flourish mentally, emotionally, and physically..

- Describe how these verses mentally coach you or help you mange your self-talk. How do these truths give you the confidence needed to walk in the good works prepared for you?

CHAPTER 5: YOU ARE A MASTERPIECE

Read 1 Peter 1:18-19

¹⁸knowing that you were not redeemed with perishable things like silver or gold from your futile way of life inherited from your forefathers, ¹⁹but with precious blood, as of a lamb unblemished and spotless, the blood of Christ."

- According to these verses, *with* what did God redeem you? *From* what did God redeem you?

- Read the insight box concerning **futile**.

- Based on passages we've looked at in previous chapters, describe how your futile way of life looked.

Futile (Mataios 3152) in the original language means devoid of truth, vain, empty, fruitless, aimless, useless, no purpose.

Zodhiates, Spiros: *The Complete Word Study Dictionary: New Testament*, electronic ed. Chattanooga, TN: AMG Publishers, ©1992, 1993, and 2000, Strongs G3152

Thayer and Smith. Greek Lexicon entry for Peripateo. The NAS New Testament Greek Lexicon 1999.

Praise be to God! You are no longer devoid of truth!

- Describe how these verses mentally coach you or help you manage your *futile (devoid of truth)* self-talk. How do these truths give you the confidence needed to walk in the good works prepared for you?

Read Psalm 34:5 (New International Version)

Those who look to him (God) are radiant; their faces are never covered with shame.

- Think about all the verses we've seen. Write below how looking to God will make you radiant.

- Describe how this verse mentally coaches you or helps you manage your *futile (devoid of truth)* self-talk. How does this scripture help you gain the confidence you need?

Read Matthew 10:29-31 (Jesus talking to His disciples)

²⁹Are not two sparrows sold for a cent? And yet not one of them will fall to the ground apart from your Father. ³⁰But the very hairs of your head are all numbered. ³¹So do not fear; you are more valuable than many sparrows.

- According to verse 30, what does Jesus know about you?

- How valuable does Jesus say you are?

- Describe how these verses mentally coach you or help you manage your self-talk. How do these truths give you the confidence needed to walk in the good works prepared for you?

CHAPTER 5: YOU ARE A MASTERPIECE

Read 1 Peter 1:3–5 (Peter is writing to those who have a relationship with Jesus)

> ³Blessed be the God and Father of our Lord Jesus Christ, who according to His great mercy has caused us to be born again to a living hope through the resurrection of Jesus Christ from the dead, ⁴to obtain an inheritance which is imperishable and undefiled and will not fade away, reserved in heaven for you, ⁵who are protected by the power of God through faith for a salvation ready to be revealed in the last time.

- According to verse 4, what do you obtain?

- How is your inheritance described?

- In verse 5, what do you learn about God's power as it relates to you and your faith?

- Describe how these verses mentally coach you or help you manage your *futile (devoid of truth)* self-talk. How do these truths give you the confidence needed to walk in the good works prepared for you?

SELF-TALK: Change your mind, change your life

Read 2 Corinthians 1:21-22

²¹Now He who establishes us with you in Christ and anointed us is God, ²²who also sealed us and gave us the Spirit in our hearts as a pledge.

Read Ephesians 1:13-14

¹³In Him, you also, after listening to the message of truth, the gospel of your salvation—having also believed, you were sealed in Him with the Holy Spirit of promise, ¹⁴who is given as a pledge of our inheritance, with a view to the redemption of God's own possession, to the praise of His glory.

Pledge (Arrabon 728) in the original language meant earnest money, a pledge, something which stands for part of the price and paid beforehand to confirm the transaction. Used in the New Testament only in a figurative sense and spoken of the Holy Spirit which God has given to believers in this present life to assure them of their future and eternal inheritance.

Zodhiates, Spiros: *The Complete Word Study Dictionary: New Testament*, Chattanooga, TN: AMG Publishers, ©1992, 1993, and 2000, Strongs G728

In modern Greek arrabon, or translated pledge in English, means engagement ring!

Sealed (Sphragizo 4972) in the original language means to set a seal or mark upon a thing as a token of its authenticity or approvedness…of Christians whom God attests and confirms by the gift of the Holy Spirit as the earnest, pledge, or seal of salvation.

Zodhiates, Spiros: *The Complete Word Study Dictionary: New Testament*, electronic ed. Chattanooga, TN: AMG Publishers, ©1992, 1993, and 2000, Strongs G4972

- Read the insight box concerning **pledge** and **sealed**.

- What do you learn about the Holy Spirit from the above verses?

- Write out below how knowing you are sealed in the Holy Spirit, who is the pledge of your inheritance, mentally coaches you or helps you manage your self-talk.

- How do these truths give you the confidence needed to walk in the good works prepared for you?

Beloved of God, no matter how you feel and no matter what the *world* has thrown, is throwing, or will throw at you or has told you, is telling you, and will tell you, the truth is that you are God's masterpiece. You were created in Christ Jesus for good works which God prepared beforehand so that you can and would walk in them—in this crazy *world*!

88

God has set His seal—the Holy Spirit—upon you. Let that truth fill your mind! God, through His Spirit, set you apart for Himself. The Holy Spirit has been given to you as a pledge from God. In a manner of speaking, you wear God's engagement ring (see previous insight box concerning the word pledge).

Think about all an engagement ring represents to the one who gives it and to the one who wears it. Being given the Holy Spirit of God is no small thing. He helps you, He teaches you, and He brings truth to your remembrance. The *world* does not have the Holy Spirit. God is not holding out on you. The devil no longer has power over you. These are all truths we'll look at in the next chapter. Page after page, we've discovered the great lengths God has gone to for us to have and be in a personal and intimate relationship with Him.

Read Galatians 2:20

I have been crucified with Christ; and it is no longer I who live, but Christ lives in me; and the life which I now live in the flesh I live by faith in the Son of God, who loved me and gave Himself up for me.

Isn't Galatians 2:20 a beautiful visual of what takes place spiritually when we declare Jesus as Lord? Our old self is crucified with Christ. It is no longer you or me that lives, but Christ lives in us! Because Christ lives in us, we now live by faith in the Son of God who loved us and gave Himself up for us. We have great value, worth and purpose. As such, we no longer live our lives doing whatever feels right.

God's Word coaches you, and mentally and emotionally prepares you for life's wild ride in this crazy *world*. Since God prepared works for you, then you need to look to Him for coaching on how to accomplish those works. Truth determines your self-talk. God's Word, God-Talk, is the final authority.

God is not asking you to deny the wild ride or the crazy that is happening to you or around you. But rather to be mentally and emotionally prepared to go out into the *world* so the *world* will believe in Jesus (John 17:15-21). You've got good works planned for you!.

Let's stop and test our self-talk against God's Word. Take a few minutes to review once again the things you wrote down about your negative body image (page 21) and your negative self-talk in Chapter 1 on page 22. Once reviewed, proceed to the self-talk quiz.

Self-Talk Quiz

The quiz is divided into five categories of self-talk. They are: (1) Body Image; (2) Value, Worth, and Purpose; (3) Circumstances; (4) The World, People, and Life; and (5) God's Word.

Within each category is a list of God-Talk—truths from God's Word we've discovered together. Add any additional Scriptures that come to mind. For each category, you will also find a list of possible self-talk. Add any self-talk not on the list.

Instructions for each category:

- Review the list of what you may be telling yourself—your self-talk (right column).
- Next, review what God says—God-talk (left column).
- Go back through your self-talk list and identify with a highlighter or underline the lies you are telling yourself and believing.
- Then identify the truths on the God-talk list that dispel the lies you have been telling yourself and believing.

" Body Image "

God-Talk: The truth about your body image

- I am God's masterpiece. (Ephesians 2:10)

- I have been created, formed and knit together by God. (Psalm 139:13)

- I am fearfully and wonderfully made by God. (Psalm 139:14)

Self-Talk: What you tell yourself about your body image

- If I change this or that (fill in the blanks) about myself I will look better and measure up.

- If only this or that about me was different (fill in the blank) I would feel better about myself and others will like me more or better.

"Value, Worth, and Purpose"

God-Talk: The truth about your value, worth, and purpose

- I have been created in Christ Jesus for good works, which God prepared beforehand so that I would walk in them. (Ephesians 2:10)
- God calls me by name and I am His. (Isaiah 43:1-4)
- God did not spare His own Son but delivered Him over for me and will freely give me all things. (Romans 8:32)
- I have an inheritance kept in heaven for me. (1 Peter 1:4)
- I am precious in God's sight. (Isaiah 43:1-4)
- I am honored by God. (Isaiah 43:1-4)
- God says . . . I LOVE YOU. (Isaiah 43:1–4)
- When I was ungodly, a sinner, an enemy of God, and helpless to do anything about it, God demonstrated His love for me by sending Jesus to die in my place. (Romans 5:6-10)
- When there was nothing lovely about me God called me Beloved. (Romans 9:25)
- God put His Holy Spirit in my heart as a deposit, guarantee, pledge of things to come. (Ephesians 1:13-14; 2 Corinthians 1:21-22)
- I have been redeemed for God's very own possession with the precious blood of Jesus. (1 Peter 1:18-19)
- God's precious thoughts toward me outnumber the grains of sand. (Psalm 139:17-18)
- God numbers every hair on my head. (Matthew 10:30)

Self-Talk: What you tell yourself about your value, worth, and purpose

- I have no real purpose.
- God could never use someone like me.
- I'll never amount to anything.
- I'm worthless.
- I have nothing.
- My life doesn't matter.
- No one loves me.
- No one cares about me.
- God has better things to do than concern Himself with me.
- I am unlovable.
- I don't measure up.
- There is nothing special about me.

 **Circumstances**

God-Talk: The truth no matter your circumstances

- God is for me. (Romans 8:31)
- God is always with me. (Psalm 139; Isaiah 43:1–4)
- God collects my tears in His bottle. (Psalm 56:8)
- God takes account of my wanderings. (Psalm 56:8)
- God is intimately acquainted with all my ways. I am never out of His sight and He knows what I am going to say before I say it. (Psalm 139)
- No one and nothing can separate me from the love of God —not tribulation, distress, persecution, famine, nakedness, peril or sword, death, life, angels, can separate me from the love of God in Christ Jesus. (Romans 8:35-39)
- I am protected by God's power through faith. (1 Peter 1:5)
- I am beloved of God. (Romans 9:25)
- God freely gives all things to me. (Romans 8:32)
- I have been reconciled to God by the death of His Son, declared right with God through Jesus' blood, and am now considered a friend of God. (Romans 5:6-10)
- When I was ungodly, a sinner, an enemy of God, and helpless to do anything about it, God demonstrated His love for me by sending me Jesus to die in my place. (Romans 5:6-10)
- In all things I overwhelmingly conquer through Him who loves me. (Romans 8:37)

Self-Talk: What you tell yourself when bad things happen

- I am all alone.
- Everyone rejects me.
- Everyone abandons me.
- God doesn't care.
- God is holding out on me.

- God is not good.

- I trusted God and look what happened.
- I can't trust God to help me.
- I am not, will not, never can be good enough.
- Bad things always happen to me.

- I can't do this anymore.

- It's too hard.

CHAPTER 5: YOU ARE A MASTERPIECE

Continued . . .

God-Talk: The truth no matter your circumstances	**Self-Talk: What you tell yourself when bad things happen**
• In Jesus, I have redemption through His blood and the forgiveness of my sins. (Ephesians 1:7)	• God will never forgive me.
• When I look to God I am radiant; my face is never covered with shame. (Psalm 34:5)	• I'll never forgive myself.
• Whatever was written in earlier times was written for my instruction, so that through perseverance and the encouragement of the Scriptures I might have hope. (Romans 15:4)	• I am so guilty and ashamed.
• Jesus prays for me. (Romans 8:34)	• God can never use me. • I have no hope.

"The World and Life in the World"

God-Talk: The truth about the world, people, and life	**Self-Talk: What you tell yourself about the world, people, and your life**
• In the world I will have troubles but I take courage because Jesus has overcome the world; there's peace in Jesus. (John 16:33)	• Bad things shouldn't happen.
• The ruler of this world is Satan (devil, serpent of old, dragon) who waged war in heaven and was thrown down to earth with his angels and deceives the whole world—including me. (John 8:44; 12:31, Revelation 12:7-9)	• I can never have peace.
• The devil is a murderer, liar. (John 8:44)	• If God were good, there would be no troubles in this world.
• Be on the alert, my adversary the devil prowls seeking to devour me and others. (1 Peter 5:8)	• There is no devil.
• Without Christ people do the desires of the devil. (John 8:44)	• There is no such thing as evil.
• Without Christ people walk according to the course of this world, according to the devil and live in and indulge in the desires of the flesh and mind. (Ephesians 2:2-3)	• The world is a good and happy place.
• All have sinned. (Romans 3:23)	• People are inheritantly good.
• Therefore, just as through one man sin entered into the world, and death through sin, and so death spread to all men, because all sinned. (Romans 5:12)	• At death I will cease to exist.
• The penalty of sin is death (eternal separation from the presence and favor of God). (Romans 6:23)	• There is no God.

Continued . . .

| **God-Talk: The truth about the world, people, and life** | **Self-Talk: What you tell yourself about the world, people, and your life** |

- For God so loved the world, that He gave Jesus so that those who believe in Him will not perish, but have eternal life (never separated from the presence and favor of God). (John 3:16)

- I live life to the fullest—my own way.

- I have been crucified with Christ; and it is no longer I who live, but Christ lives in me; and the life which I now live in the flesh I live by faith in the Son of God, who loved me and gave Himself up for me. (Galatians 2:20)

- How I live doesn't matter.

- Declaring Jesus as Lord means I've been redeemed from my futile way of life (and thinking) with the precious blood of Christ. (1 Peter 18-19)

- What I think and tell myself doesn't matter.

"God's Word"

God-Talk: The truth about God's Word

- God's Word is truth. (John 17:17).
- God's Word—truth—is my only weapon against the lies of the world and the evil one. (Ephesians 6:17).
- God means what he says. What he says goes. His powerful Word is sharp as a surgeon's scalpel, cutting through everything, whether doubt or defense, laying us open to listen and obey. Nothing and no one is impervious to God's Word. We can't get away from it—no matter what. (Hebrews 4:12-13 - The Message)
- God's Word is eternal and stands firm in the heavens. (Psalm 119:89 - NIV)
- All scripture is inspired by God and profitable for teaching, reproof, for correction, for training in righteousness; so that the man of God may be adequate, equipped for every good work. (2 Timothy 3:16-17)
- The sum of or all of God's Word is true. (Psalm 119:160)
- No prophecy of Scripture is a matter of one's interpretation—no prophecy was made by an act of human will, but men moved by the Holy Spirit spoke from God. (2 Peter 1:20-21

Self-Talk: What you tell yourself about God's Word

- Truth is relative.
- There is no absolute truth.
- The Bible is outdated and irrelevant.
- Times and cultures change.
- Scripture contains errors, inconsistencies and contradictions.
- I can't understand the Bible.
- The Bible is a book of stories.
- Every religion leads to the same place.
- What I tell myself and others doesn't matter.

CHAPTER 5: YOU ARE A MASTERPIECE

To whose word will you or do you yield?

Let me repeat something I said earlier. The first step in being mentally and emotionally prepared to walk in the work God has prepared for you is this—get your mind fully wrapped around the fact that you truly are God's masterpiece created in Christ Jesus.

You are beloved of God! Believe it. Remind yourself daily. Set this truth as a 7 pm daily reminder on your phone. Let truth give you the confidence and knowledge needed to walk out into the crazy *world* and accomplish the good works that God planned beforehand for you. The *world* needs you because the *world* needs Jesus.

> **7 PM REMINDER**
>
> I am God's masterpiece created in Christ Jesus to do good works.

Now that you have identified the lies you are telling yourself and believing, stop and pray. Allow God to wash you in His Word until it changes your mind and the way you think and live. You know how a long hot shower washes off the sweat, dirt, and grime after a run, workout, or day of gardening? It's like that. Let the Word of God wash over you until your self-talk matches God's talk. Wash in the Word until your heart matches God's heart for you and until God's Word changes how you think and live.

Now that you understand how to use God's Word to coach and mentally and emotionally prepare yourself, let's look at what it looks like to walk (live) and work in the *world*.

#6 Walking and Working in the World

Holy in truth

In the span of one short week, many of our friends experienced great sorrow. We went to the funeral of one of our neighbors. He and his wife were married 55 years. While my husband and I can try to comfort her by bringing food and checking on her, there is no way to ease her sorrow.

The evening of the funeral, I got a message from a dear, young friend of mine that her mother had died. As we spent the next day with her, we learned that her mom didn't have, or seemingly want, a relationship with her and her brother. The story and circumstances were heartbreaking.

As I was drying my tears for her, I received a call that another friend who, seven weeks pregnant with twins, was having a miscarriage. Sitting in the hospital listening to the doctor tell this precious soul that the babies she had just lost weren't considered babies was horrifying.

As I wept and prayed for my friends, my heart was troubled and overwhelmed. I know my prayers and being there and doing the small things were a comfort, but how I longed to take away their suffering. It's a horrible and helpless feeling. I know these were precious moments to love on people in Jesus name—moments God prepared for me beforehand. But at times like this, it's hard to make sense of suffering. I had to keep reminding myself of God's Word and let it wash over me. I had to keep letting God's Word coach me. Wave after wave of sorrow took mental management on my part because my thinking was getting off. Why? I don't want a *world* filled with troubles. It's emotionally exhausting. I just want God to fix everything. It's all too hard, it hurts too much, and there goes my thinking.

As I was talking to the Lord about all these sorrows and troubles, I realized that I needed to get a grip on the strong bar of God's Word. I needed to let God talk to me. As I turned to God's Word, Jesus' last words to His disciples came to mind. Actually, I am sure the Holy Spirit brought them to mind. Oh, this is a wonderful truth for us to stop and explore.

For the fun of discovery, keep watching and marking the words listed for you before each Scripture reference.

Draw a circle around *world*.

Draw a star through *word*.

Draw a heart through *believe*.

Read John 17:15-21 (Jesus' final prayer)

> [15]I do not ask You to take them out of the world, but to keep them from the evil one. [16]They are not of the world, even as I am not of the world. [17]Sanctify them in the truth; Your word is truth. [18]As You sent Me into the world, I also have sent them into the world. [19] For their sakes I sanctify Myself, that they themselves also may be sanctified in truth. [20]I do not ask on behalf of these alone, but for those also who believe in Me through their word; [21]that they may all be one; even as You, Father, are in Me and I in You, that they also may be in Us, so that the world may believe that You sent Me.

Reread verse 16 again. In the *world* but not of the *world*. Hold that thought.

It is a grand and glorious truth that we are God's masterpiece, created in Christ Jesus. Before God spoke the *world* into existence, He thought of you and planned and prepared good works for you. Let's read Ephesians 2:10 again.

Read Ephesians 2:10

For we are His (God's) workmanship, created in Christ Jesus for good works, which God prepared beforehand so that we would walk in them.

The New Living Translations says: "For we are God's masterpiece...".

Then comes the "walk in them" part. This means to walk and work in the crazy *world* while being different and not part of the *world*. And let's not forget the troubles we will have in this *world*, and we'll talk about those in detail in the next chapter. For now, let's focus on this. Just in case you haven't noticed, walking (in the good works prepared beforehand for us) and working in the *world* is going to be challenging.

In the *world*, but not of the *world*. Walking and working as holy and set apart for God. Holy among the unholy.

What does it mean to be holy?

Great question. What does it mean for people to be holy? For some, this thought could evoke terror and for others confusion. Does it mean we are going to wear halos, robes, go to church every day and listen to organ music? Does it mean we become so holy that we separate ourselves from the *world* living like monks?

Before our minds run off in too many directions, remember Jesus. He humbled Himself for people. He loved people. Remember also, for God so loved the *world* that He sent His only son. He says we are to be in the *world*, but not of the *world*. How is this possible? Let's examine together what Jesus is saying.

Read John 17:17

Sanctify them in the truth; Your word is truth.

Read John 17:17 (New Living Translation)

Make them holy by your truth; teach them your word, which is truth.

- Read the insight box concerning **sanctify**.
- According to verse 17, how are you made holy or set apart in your thinking, values, attitudes, and behavior from the *world*?

- What does Jesus say truth is?

Sanctify (Hagiazo 37) in the original language means to make holy, set apart from a common to a sacred use. Spoken of persons, to consecrate as being set apart of God and sent by Him for the performance of His will.

Zodiates, Spiros: *The Complete Word Study Dictionary: New Testament*, electronic ed. Chattanooga, TN:AMG Publishers, ©1992, 1993, and 2000 Strongs G37

As a well-loved child of God, it's important for you to know that you've already been declared holy and set apart unto God (1 Peter 2:9). This is a marvelous and amazing truth. So then, what does it mean to be holy or set apart for God?

To be holy means truth has authority over your thoughts, values, attitudes, and behaviors. As a result, your thoughts, values, attitudes, and behaviors are different than those of the *world*. No longer are you futile (devoid of truth) in your thinking (1 Peter 1:18-19).

> **To be holy means truth has authority over your thoughts, values, attitudes, and behaviors. As a result, your thoughts, values, attitudes, and behaviors are different than those of the world.**

For example, this is what we were doing in the last chapter as we examined our self-talk and what we tell ourselves against God-talk, the truth. We examined God's Word and found that truth exposed the lies we tell ourselves and believe. The truth of God's Word challenges and changes the way we think—our values, our attitudes, and our behavior.

But we cannot walk holy if we don't know truth, and if we don't talk truth for ourselves we cannot walk holy.

CHAPTER 6: WALKING AND WORKING IN THE WORLD

To be holy means we think, talk, walk, and work according to what God says rather than according to what you tell yourself, or according to the *world*.

- Before we go further, describe what you currently tell yourself concerning being holy.

- Now, describe what it means to be holy based on God's Word.

As beloved children of God, we've been set apart unto God, and now we are to set ourselves apart, be made holy, by being in God's Word. We are to fill our minds with truth. Once totally devoid of truth, we now know and understand that God's Word is vital if we are to be holy.

Read Hebrews 4:12

For the word of God is living and active and sharper than any two-edged sword, and piercing as far as the division of soul and spirit, of both joints and marrow, and able to judge the thoughts and intentions of the heart.

God's Word is powerful. Truth pierces and judges our thoughts and the intentions of our heart. God has given us His Word, so we are no longer devoid of truth. And He gives us a Helper to help us walk in truth.

Talk of being holy should not send the emotions or voices of *Fear*, *Guilt*, and *Shame* screaming in your head. Jesus says we can be made holy! We can be made holy or sanctify ourselves in the truth. God's Word is truth. And here is the best news and most important truth. As well-loved children of God, we have been given the Holy Spirit of God to help us. Keep reading and marking because there is truth treasure to discover!

SELF-TALK: Change your mind, change your life

Your Helper in the *world*

Circle references to ***world***.

Draw an **arrow** through ***Helper*** or ***Spirit of Truth*** including pronouns and synonyms.

Read John 14:16-21 (Jesus talking)

> ¹⁶I will ask the Father, and He will give you another Helper, that He may be with you forever; ¹⁷that is the Spirit of truth, whom the world cannot receive, because it does not see Him or know Him, but you know Him because He abides with you and will be in you. ¹⁸I will not leave you as orphans; I will come to you. ¹⁹After a little while the world will no longer see Me, but you will see Me; because I live, you will live also. ²⁰In that day you will know that I am in My Father, and you in Me, and I in you. ²¹He who has My commandments and keeps them is the one who loves Me; and he who loves Me will be loved by My Father, and I will love him and will disclose Myself to him.

Abide (Meno 3306) in the original language means to remain, abide, dwell, live. Of a person remaining or dwelling in a place.

Zodhiates, Spiros: *The Complete Word Study Dictionary: New Testament*, electronic ed. Chattanooga, TN: AMG Publishers, ©1992, 1993, and 2000, Strongs G3306

- Look back over your arrows. What is another name for the Helper?

- According to verse 17, how do you know the Helper?

- Read the insight box concerning **abide**.

- In your own words, explain the significance of having the Spirit of Truth abiding with you and in you?

- Who cannot receive the Spirit of Truth?

CHAPTER 6: WALKING AND WORKING IN THE WORLD

Circle references to **world**.

Draw an **arrow** through **Helper** or **Holy Spirit** including pronouns and synonyms.

Read John 14:25-27 (Jesus speaking)

²⁵These things I have spoken to you while abiding with you. ²⁶But the Helper, the Holy Spirit, whom the Father will send in My name, He will teach you all things, and bring to your remembrance all that I said to you. ²⁷Peace I leave with you; My peace I give to you; not as the world gives do I give to you. Do not let your heart be troubled, nor let it be fearful.

- What is another name for the Helper?

- According to verses 25-26, what is the role of the Holy Spirit in your life?

- In verse 27, what does Jesus say He gives you?

- Describe the impact His peace given to you has on your self-talk as well as your holy walk and work in the *world*.

- How does this verse help you mentally manage being afraid?

Read John 16:13(a)

But when He, the Spirit of truth, comes, He will guide you into all the truth.

- According to John 16:13, what is the role of the Holy Spirit?

- How will the Holy Spirit teach you, call God's Word to remembrance, or guide you into *all* truth if you do not know or are not spending time in God's Word?

- Are you willing to allow the Holy Spirit to guide you into all truth? Think about it before you answer. Truth taught by the Holy Spirit could challenge what you have believed to be true. If so, don't panic! Just be willing to allow the Holy Spirit to guide you into all truth and trust God to work out that truth in your heart and walk. So are you willing to allow the Holy Spirit to guide you into all truth?

- Explain how having the Word of God and the Holy Spirit abiding in you enables you to think and thus be holy.

Draw an **arrow** through **Spirit**.

Read Galatians 5:16, 19-25

[16]But I say, walk by the Spirit, and you will not carry out the desire of the flesh.

[19] Now the deeds of the flesh are evident, which are: immorality, impurity, sensuality, [20]idolatry, sorcery, enmities, strife, jealousy, outbursts of anger, disputes, dissensions, factions, [21]envying, drunkenness, carousing, and things like these, of which I forewarn you, just as I have forewarned you, that those who practice such things will not inherit the kingdom of God. [22]But the fruit of the Spirit is love, joy, peace, patience, kindness, goodness, faithfulness, [23]gentleness, self-control; against such things there is no law. [24]Now those who belong to Christ Jesus have crucified the flesh with its passions and desires. [25]If we live by the Spirit, let us also walk by the Spirit.

CHAPTER 6: WALKING AND WORKING IN THE WORLD

- How does the Holy Spirit help you according to Galatians 5:16 and 25?

- According to verses 19-21, what are the deeds of the flesh?

Ephesians 2:1-3 tells us that before Christ, we lived in the lusts of our flesh and indulged in the desires of our flesh and mind. These were the things we practiced as a habit or way of life. As such, we were walking according to the course of this *world* and according to the ruler of this *world*. Remember? The deeds of the flesh are the way of the *world*. That was our old life. Our futile (devoid of truth) way of life (1 Peter 1:18-19). In stark contrast, God desires for us walk holy in truth. What would that look like in the *world* to walk and be holy? Go back and read Galatians 5:22-25 (page 106).

- According to verses 22-24, what does it look like to live or walk by the Spirit?

- Based on all the passages of Scriptures we've read, if you are not carrying out the desires of the flesh, would you be walking by the Spirit and be living holy and set apart? Would you be different from the *world*?

- Based on all the Scriptures we've examined, explain how you can be holy.

Your holy walk in the *world*

Change your mind, change your life, and change the *world*! You are to set yourself apart from the world in thinking, values, attitudes, and behavior in the truth. You fill your mind with God's Word so that the Holy Spirit can teach and guide you into all truth. You have the Word of God and the Holy Spirit of God dwelling and living inside of you to help you be holy. As you set yourself apart, God will do a supernatural work in your mind and heart through the power of His Word and His Spirit. Because of this, you can be holy and set apart in your thinking, values, attitudes, and behaviors. In the *world*, but not of the *world*, so that the *world* might believe in Jesus. Let's look at these words from Jesus one more time.

Read John 17:15-21

> [15]*I do not ask You to take them out of the world, but to keep them from the evil one.* [16]*They are not of the world, even as I am not of the world.* [17]*Sanctify them in the truth; Your word is truth.* [18]*As You sent Me into the world, I also have sent them into the world.* [19]*For their sakes I sanctify Myself, that they themselves also may be sanctified in truth.* [20]*I do not ask on behalf of these alone, but for those also who believe in Me through their word;* [21]*that they may all be one; even as You, Father, are in Me and I in You, that they also may be in Us, so that the world may believe that You sent Me.*

- Based on verse 20, how do you know Jesus is praying this for you?

- According to verses 20-21, what is Jesus asking the Father to do in and through you?

- Based on all the Scriptures we've examined, explain to yourself why it is important to be holy. What is the point and purpose of being holy?

CHAPTER 6: WALKING AND WORKING IN THE WORLD

In the *world,* but not of the *world,* so that the *world* might believe in Jesus. Wow! What an amazing purpose God has for our walking and working in the world - holy in truth!

Let's take the rest of this chapter to explore passages from God's Word that contrast what it means to walk in the flesh as children of the devil (darkness), versus walking by the Spirit as children of God (light). These contrasts in behavior are stark. We will see clearly what is *world*ly or unholy behavior and what is godly or holy behavior. Let's look at these contrasts together.

Read Ephesians 4:1-3, 14-32 (talking to believers about their walk in the *world*, how they relate to each other, the role and purpose of the church, etc.)

> ¹Therefore I, the prisoner of the Lord, implore you to walk in a manner worthy of the calling with which you have been called, ²with all humility and gentleness, with patience, showing tolerance for one another in love, ³being diligent to preserve the unity of the Spirit in the bond of peace.
>
> ¹⁴As a result, we are no longer to be children, tossed here and there by waves and carried about by every wind of doctrine, by the trickery of men, by craftiness in deceitful scheming; ¹⁵but speaking the truth in love, we are to grow up in all aspects into Him who is the head, even Christ, ¹⁶from whom the whole body, being fitted and held together by what every joint supplies, according to the proper working of each individual part, causes the growth of the body for the building up of itself in love. ¹⁷So this I say, and affirm together with the Lord, that you walk no longer just as the Gentiles also walk, in the futility of their mind, ¹⁸being darkened in their understanding, excluded from the life of God because of the ignorance that is in them, because of the hardness of their heart; ¹⁹and they, having become callous, have given themselves over to sensuality for the practice of every kind of impurity with greediness. ²⁰But you did not learn Christ in this way, ²¹if indeed you have heard Him and have been taught in Him, just as truth is in Jesus, ²²that, in reference to your former manner of life, you lay aside the old self, which is being corrupted in accordance with the lusts of deceit, ²³and that you be renewed in the spirit of your mind, ²⁴and put on the new self, which in the likeness of God has been created in righteousness and holiness of the truth ²⁵Therefore, laying aside falsehood, SPEAK TRUTH EACH ONE of you WITH HIS NEIGHBOR, for we are members of one another. ²⁶BE ANGRY, AND yet DO NOT SIN; do not let the sun go down on your anger, ²⁷and do not give the devil an opportunity. ²⁸He who steals must steal no longer; but rather he must labor, performing with his own hands what is good, so that he will have something to share with one who has need. ²⁹Let no unwholesome word proceed from your mouth, but only such a word as is good for edification according to the need of the moment, so that it will give grace to those who hear. ³⁰Do not grieve the Holy Spirit of God, by whom you were sealed for the day of redemption. ³¹Let all bitterness and wrath and anger and clamor and slander be put away from you, along with all malice. ³²Be kind to one another, tender-hearted, forgiving each other, just as God in Christ also has forgiven you.

CHAPTER 6: WALKING AND WORKING IN THE WORLD

- Based on these verses, list examples of what is holy behavior and what is unholy behavior.

Holy Behavior (not of the *world*)	**Unholy Behavior** (of the *world*)

Now that you have taken the time to lists these truths and have spent all these chapters exploring and pondering truths from God's Word, are you starting to see things God's way? Do you see truth?

Are you changing your mind?

We come into this *world* in bodies of flesh and with *world*ly desires, ways, and thoughts. We are deceived and distorted in our thinking. We are dead in our sins. Our relationship with Jesus changes everything for us. Through the power of God's Word and the Holy Spirit, God is going to supernaturally change our thinking, values, attitudes, and behavior so that the *world* would know Jesus.

Holy = life and all things good. Unholy = death and all things destructive.

These passages from Ephesians, as well as the passages that follow, coach us on how to live our daily lives. They give us wisdom on how to behave, what to say, and how relate to and with others. Let's do this—referring back to the list you just made from Ephesians of holy and unholy behaviors, answer the following questions.

- When someone is rude to you, cuts you off in traffic, gives poor customer service and any number of irritating things happen to you, what does holy look like?

- When people get on your last nerve and you want to vent to someone in person or via social media, what can you stop and remember before saying (writing) anything?

CHAPTER 6: WALKING AND WORKING IN THE WORLD

- What do verses 17-19 teach you about the behaviors of sensuality, impurity and greed?

- In general, what motivates you to want to stop and remember or walk and behave as holy?

- Based on these verses, why is your holy behavior important and what difference does holy behavior make in the *world*? Remember also John 17:15-21.

Read Ephesians 5:1-17 (talking to believers about their walk in the *world*, how they relate to each other, the role and purpose of the church, etc.)

¹Therefore be imitators of God, as beloved children; ²and walk in love, just as Christ also loved you and gave Himself up for us, an offering and a sacrifice to God as a fragrant aroma. ³But immorality or any impurity or greed must not even be named among you, as is proper among saints; ⁴and there must be no filthiness and silly talk, or coarse jesting, which are not fitting, but rather giving of thanks. ⁵For this you know with certainty, that no immoral or impure person or covetous man, who is an idolater, has an inheritance in the kingdom of Christ and God. ⁶Let no one deceive you with empty words, for because of these things the wrath of God comes upon the sons of disobedience. ⁷Therefore do not be partakers with them; ⁸for you were formerly darkness, but now you are Light in the Lord; walk as children of Light ⁹(for the fruit of the Light consists in all goodness and righteousness and truth), ¹⁰trying to learn what is pleasing to the Lord. ¹¹Do not participate in the unfruitful deeds of darkness, but instead even expose them; ¹²for it is disgraceful even to speak of the things which are done by them in secret. ¹³But all things become visible when they are exposed by the light, for everything that becomes visible is light. ¹⁴For this reason it says,

"Awake, sleeper,
And arise from the dead,
And Christ will shine on you."

¹⁵Therefore be careful how you walk, not as unwise men but as wise, ¹⁶making the most of your time, because the days are evil. ¹⁷So then do not be foolish, but understand what the will of the Lord is.

- Based on these verses, list examples of what is holy behavior and what is unholy behavior.

CHAPTER 6: WALKING AND WORKING IN THE WORLD

Holy Behavior (not of the *world*)	**Unholy Behavior** (of the *world*)

Using the list of holy and unholy behavior, answer the following questions.

- In what ways does this Ephesians 5:1-17 teach or coach you on how a beloved child of God behaves or what it looks like to imitate God?

- On which list do you find gossip and slander, and what does this show you about participating in gossip or slander?

- What does this passage teach and coach you about behaviors like sexual immorality, dirty stories or jokes, and foolish or silly talk?

- According to verses 15-17,
  How are you coached to walk or behave?

  How are you to spend your time?

  Why is making the most of your time important?

  How are you able to walk as wise and not be foolish?

CHAPTER 6: WALKING AND WORKING IN THE WORLD

- In general, what motivates you to want to walk and behave as holy?

- Based on these verses, explain why your holy behavior is important and what difference your holy behavior will make in the *world*? Remember also John 17:15-21.

Read Colossians 3:5-17 (talking to believers about their walk in the *world*, how they relate to each other)

⁵*Therefore, consider the members of your earthly body as dead to immorality, impurity, passion, evil desire, and greed, which amounts to idolatry. ⁶For it is because of these things that the wrath of God will come upon the sons of disobedience, ⁷and in them you also once walked, when you were living in them. ⁸But now you also, put them all aside: anger, wrath, malice, slander, and abusive speech from your mouth. ⁹Do not lie to one another, since you laid aside the old self with its evil practices, ¹⁰and have put on the new self who is being renewed to a true knowledge according to the image of the One who created him—¹¹a renewal in which there is no distinction between Greek and Jew, circumcised and uncircumcised, barbarian, Scythian, slave and freeman, but Christ is all, and in all. ¹²So, as those who have been chosen of God, holy and beloved, put on a heart of compassion, kindness, humility, gentleness and patience; ¹³bearing with one another, and forgiving each other, whoever has a complaint against anyone; just as the Lord forgave you, so also should you. ¹⁴Beyond all these things put on love, which is the perfect bond of unity. ¹⁵Let the peace of Christ rule in your hearts, to which indeed you were called in one body; and be thankful. ¹⁶Let the word of Christ richly dwell within you, with all wisdom teaching and admonishing one another with psalms and hymns and spiritual songs, singing with thankfulness in your hearts to God. ¹⁷Whatever you do in word or deed, do all in the name of the Lord Jesus, giving thanks through Him to God the Father.*

CHAPTER 6: WALKING AND WORKING IN THE WORLD

- Based on these verses, list examples of what is holy behavior and what is unholy behavior.

Holy Behavior (not of the *world*)	**Unholy Behavior** (of the *world*)

Using the list of holy and unholy behavior, answer the following questions.

- What does verse 10 teach and coach you to do?

- In what ways does the first part of verse 12 remind you and motivate you to "put on?"

- Re-read verses 15 and 16. What do you learn about the peace of Christ and the Word of God?

- In general, what motivates you to want to walk and behave as holy?

There is a huge difference between the way the children of God think and act and how the children of the devil think and act. Walking in holiness is in stark contrast to walking according to the *world*. Those in

CHAPTER 6: WALKING AND WORKING IN THE WORLD

the *world* are devoid of truth and have no Helper. But, they have you!

So that the *world* might believe

Read 2 Corinthians 5:20

Therefore, we are ambassadors for Christ, as though God were making an appeal through us; we beg you on behalf of Christ, be reconciled to God.

What an inspiring verse. Think about the privilege and responsibility you have been given to testify to the *world* the truth about Jesus. You are in this *world*, so the *world* might believe in Jesus. An ambassador for Christ, as though God were making an appeal through you, begging the *world* to be reconciled to Him. You—begging the *world* to go from being an enemy of God to a friend of God because of the precious blood of Jesus.

Please remember God has given you everything you need to be holy. You have His precious Word, and you have the Holy Spirit. Being holy in the *world* is a supernatural, God-given ability. Being holy isn't a "to-do" list of behaviors that you muster-up so you can be on the "good list" or check off the list. You don't act kind because it's on the list. You are kind because you can and have put on a heart of kindness.

> **Being holy starts with your intimate relationship with Jesus and flows out of your relationship with God's Word and the Holy Spirit abiding in you. It's relational.**

Being holy starts with your intimate relationship with Jesus and flows out of your relationship with God's Word and the Holy Spirit abiding in you. It's relational. Being holy takes your participation but requires God's enabling. Because of your relationship, that of a well-loved child, you want to imitate God.

- Based on all we've looked at in this chapter, summarize again for yourself why your holy behavior is important and what difference holy behavior will make in the *world*.

You are not of the *world* but sent into the *world*

It's a crazy *world* alright, filled with people acting crazy. This once was true of us. Sure, we may still have our crazy moments, but no longer are we devoid of truth. We do not have to live in a fog of deception. The Spirit of Truth teaches and guides and certainly makes it clear why Jesus says that in this *world* we will have troubles. The people in the *world* need Jesus.

The people in the *world* need you to show them, Jesus. Not just tell them about Jesus, but show them Jesus by the way you behave. The *world* needs to see what it looks like to have a personal and intimate relationship with Jesus. The most important work you can do is be made holy in the truth and keep on being made holy until you take your final breath.

Let God's Word, through the power of the Holy Spirit abiding in you, wash over you, cleanse you, and wash away the *world*. The result—your thinking, values, attitudes, and behaviors will be made holy. Let your word, your walk, and your work in the *world* be holy in truth. Imitate God.

Please go to the appendix. Placed there for you is a beautiful picture of what it looks like to walk and work in the *world*—holy in truth. It's beautiful. You will want to be part of this kind of community. Others will be drawn to it and will also want to be a part of it. This community is possible because its people have a personal and intimate relationship with Jesus and as such have the Word of God and the Spirit of God abiding within. Holy in truth. In the *world* but not of the *world*. It all starts with you!

#7 The Truth about Trouble

Wait for it

As with the other six chapters or truths, knowing and telling yourself this seventh truth should and will change your mind, your self-talk, and thus change your life. Each one of these truths builds upon the other. You need to know and tell yourself the first one before you move on to the second one, and so forth. Getting your mind around the six other truths is imperative before you can truly grasp the truth about trouble.

When trouble comes, what do you tell yourself? For instance, does trouble cause you to revert back to any of your default negative self-talk listed in Chapter 1? Write out below what you usually tell yourself when troubles, trials, difficulties, and suffering come your way.

- What is your self-talk when it comes to troubles, trials, difficulties, and sufferings?

Guess what? God has a lot to say in His Word about troubles. What He has to say is totally different than what I told myself about and during troubles. But I could never seem to get my mind around the truth about trouble until I first got my mind around the previous chapters I've just shared with you.

Learning to understand and mentally and emotionally manage trouble is crucial to accomplishing our God given purpose in the *world*. As God's well-loved children, as people who are in a personal and intimate relationship with our Heavenly Father, we need to fill our minds with what His Word to us says about our troubles.

Because trouble can make us react in truth and be holy or trouble can make us think and act crazy, let's get right to the point of this chapter.

Read Romans 8:28

And we know that God causes all things to work together for good to those who love God, to those who are called according to His purpose.

- According to this passage, how many things work together for good?

All things would include trouble. Right? If you want to shut down right now, please don't. Wait for it... Don't miss that God, in His Word, shows us how He uses the troubles we will have in this *world* for our good. Remember, you have the Holy Spirit to teach you, guide you, and give you the supernatural ability to walk in the truth about trouble. Let's just see what God says.

Here's the first example of how God uses trouble for your good.

Troubles prove your faith is real

Read 1 Peter 1:3-9

³Blessed be the God and Father of our Lord Jesus Christ, who according to His great mercy has caused us to be born again to a living hope through the resurrection of Jesus Christ from the dead ⁴to obtain an inheritance which is imperishable and undefiled and will not fade away, reserved in heaven for you, ⁵who are protected by the power of God through faith for a salvation ready to be revealed in the last time. ⁶In this you greatly rejoice, even though now for a little while, if necessary, you have been distressed by various trials, ⁷so that the proof of your faith, being more precious

CHAPTER 7: THE TRUTH ABOUT TROUBLE

than gold which is perishable, even though tested by fire, may be found to result in praise and glory and honor at the revelation of Jesus Christ; ⁸and though you have not seen Him, you love Him, and though you do not see Him now, but believe in Him, you greatly rejoice with joy inexpressible and full of glory, ⁹obtaining as the outcome of your faith the salvation of your souls.

- According to verses 6-7:
  What is being or has been tested by fire?

  Read the insight box concerning **proof**.
  What proves your faith is genuine?

> **Proof** (Dokimion 1383) in the original language means proving, a criterion or test by which anything is proved or tried, as faith by afflictions. Here referring to genuineness or approved quality of faith.
>
> Zodhiates, Spiros: *The Complete Word Study Dictionary: New Testament*, electronic ed. Chattanooga, TN: AMG Publishers, ©1992, 1993, and 2000, Strongs G1383

- What do your troubles tell you and the *world* about your faith?

- According to this passage, how does God use trouble for good in your life?

- In what ways does this verse coach you and help you mentally prepare and understand why you can "greatly rejoice" in trials?

No, you don't deny your emotions. The emotional characters of *Sadness, Fear,* and all the others are still there, and trouble gets them screaming and running crazy. No, this verse is not saying be Pollyannaish[1]. No, greatly rejoicing doesn't mean the testing is any less difficult or painful. But in the difficulty and pain, good will come. Because your faith is being proven real and genuine, you greatly rejoice. Let me give you an example.

After Tom and I had realized we would not be able to have children of our own, we decided to pursue adoption. After the baby was born, the young woman changed her mind, and we were devastated. All these years later, I remember that day and the pain as though it was yesterday. I could go on for pages and pages about the experience and why other options weren't available to us and thus our dreams of having children were shattered. But that's not where I want to go with this story. The point of this story is how my faith was being tested.

Over 30 years ago, I was devastated and needed answers from God. Nothing made sense to me. It was a test of my faith for sure. I prayed, and I read, and I searched.

It wasn't long until I discovered Jeremiah 29:11 which says, *"For I know the plans that I have for you, declares the LORD, plans for welfare and not for calamity to give you a future and a hope."*

I clung to my faith that God is good and that His plans for me are good. While I waited for those plans to include children, I continued to search God's Word. Where else could I go with all my pain and hurt but to the One who had all the answers to all the questions I had. As I have already shared with you, the more I searched, the more I got to know my God and my Jesus.

Years later, I discovered the passages that followed Jeremiah 29:11, and as I read them I laughed, and I cried. Verses 12-14(a) says: *"Then you will call upon Me and come and pray to Me, and I will listen to you. You will seek Me and find Me when you search for Me with all your heart. I will be found by you."*

I could write an entire book on how that specific trouble brought me to this very point in my life in my walk and relationship with Jesus and God's Word. I searched for Him in the pages of His Book with all of my heart, and I found Him. I searched for Him and found Him in a way I know that I would not have without that trouble. That trouble was a huge test of my faith that grew my faith.

I recently heard Beth Moore beautifully express what I am trying to share with you. She said, "There is something more powerful than our pain and that is God making Himself known to us."

More powerful than my pain of not having children was God making Himself known to me in very personal ways. In this I greatly rejoice. God continues to make Himself known to me. In testing and growing my faith, He helped me to understand some very specific good works in which He had prepared for me to walk in. In that one trouble and great loss, God taught me the value of being a spiritual mother and gave me the privilege of "birthing" spiritual things.

Over these 30 years, He made sure to point out the good He is making out of that trouble by tying it into specific dates, names, cities, and details that only He could orchestrate. It is a sweetness from and with the Lord that I cannot explain. I do not want you to miss the good God will bring from your sufferings that test your faith. I do not deny the feelings of loss. In fact, I still have moments of mourning motherhood, but I can greatly rejoice in this suffering because of good that God has brought and will bring as a result of this trouble.

He is more powerful than our pain. He is a wonder.

Trouble proves your faith is real. God will bring good from trouble. Search for Him, look for Him, expect to be found by Him. Wait for it…

SELF-TALK: Change your mind, change your life

Trouble tests your faith, produces endurance and results in holiness.

Consider - make up your mind ahead of time².

Joy - choosing to live above feelings while not denying feelings. Keep sense of joy in midst of sorrow².

Endure - Remain under without looking for an escape or shortcut².

Draw a **jagged line** through references to **endurance**.
Draw a **heart** through **faith**.

Read James 1:2-4

> ²Consider it all joy, my brethren, when you encounter various trials, ³knowing that the testing of your faith produces endurance. ⁴And let endurance have its perfect result, so that you may be perfect and complete, lacking in nothing.

- Read the insight box concerning **consider, joy**, and **endure**.
- Read the insight box concerning **trial**.
- Using these definitions, write out what it means to consider it all joy when you encounter various trials:

- Write down how various trials have tested your faith.

Trial (Peirasmos 3986) in the original language means trial, temptation, a putting to the test, spoken of persons only. When God is the agent, it is for the purpose of proving someone, never for the purpose of causing him to fall. If it is the devil who tempts then it is for the purpose of causing one to fall.

Zodhiates, Spiros: *The Complete Word Study Dictionary: New Testament,* electronic ed. Chattanooga, TN: AMG Publishers, ©1992, 1993, and 2000, Strongs G3986

- Based on verse 3, what does the testing of your faith produce?

- Based on verses 2 and 3, why should you consider it all joy when you encounter various trials? Be sure to reference what you wrote earlier using the definitions of consider and joy.

CHAPTER 7: THE TRUTH ABOUT TROUBLE

- Read the insight box concerning **complete**.

- Based on verse 4, what is the result of endurance?

- Using this verse, talk truth to yourself. Write out what you need to remember when trouble comes, what's happening, how is God using it and what will be the result? Testify truth to yourself.

Complete (Holokleros 2648) in the original language expresses the perfection of man before the fall. Free from sin, faultless.

Zodhiates, Spiros: *The Complete Word Study Dictionary: New Testament*, electronic ed. Chattanooga, TN:AMG Publishers, ©1992, 1993, 2000, Strongs G2648

Thayer and Smith. Greek Lexicon entry for Peripateo. The NAS New Testament Greek Lexicon 1999.

On a human level, nothing about a trial says joy. But on a spiritual level, God is using your trial to grow your faith and shape and make you into the good and godly beloved child He intends you to be.

Consider it all joy when you encounter various trials. *Joy, did you hear that?* If you watched the movie *Inside Out*, the emotional character of *Joy* spent most of the movie trying to keep *Sadness* out of the main character of Riley's emotions. By the end of the movie, *Joy* realized the important role *Sadness* played in making Riley who she was. *Joy* then embraced *Sadness*, and they worked as a team. At that moment, the movie *Inside Out* preached James 1:2-4.

As you and I encounter various trials, our faith will be tested because we need to learn to be holy and set apart in our thinking and behavior. Our thinking will get tested. Our holy walk and behavior will be tested. We'll have multiple opportunities to learn how to be holy, practice being holy, learn how to walk and live by the Spirit, and practice walking and living by the Spirit.

We endure our trials and troubles without looking for an escape or shortcut because learning to be holy and being holy is good! It's part of being a beloved child of God and living out our God given purpose for the *world* to witness. Our holy behavior, especially when experiencing trouble, is the *good* this evil *world* needs to see.

God uses trouble to test our faith. The testing of our faith produces endurance resulting in holiness. Let endurance have its perfect result. God will cause it to work together for good. Search for it, look for it, expect it and wait for it…

Trouble trains you in holiness

I have never trained for a race, but I have talked to runners about their training schedule. They lay aside many things so they can stay focused. They train no matter the weather, body aches or even minor injuries. They let endurance have its perfect result.

Years ago, I watched a woman running a marathon and pushing herself beyond her physical limits. Toward the end of the race, she could barely put one leg in front of the other. She fell and got back up on her feet multiple times. She lost bodily functions. It was not pretty, but she kept on going. I couldn't believe it. Nothing was going to stop her. She had her eyes fixed on the finish line. I was amazed at her determination.

I wonder: "As beloved children of God, shouldn't we pursue imitating our Heavenly Father with the same laser like focus and determination?" Of course, we should. But training takes a lot of discipline. And, let's face it, we must see the value in training.

Personally, I see no value in training to run a marathon, half marathon, or even a 5K race. Therefore, I will never train to run. If I see no value in imitating God to a crazy *world*, I will never endure the training needed to be holy, or to go on and actually be holy.

- On a scale of 1 (no value) to 10 (most valuable), what value do you place on being holy or imitating God? Be honest.

  1   2   3   4   5   6   7   8   9   10

Trouble tests our faith and produces endurance, and endurance results in our holiness. We are in need of endurance because in this *world* we will have troubles. That is what it takes to train to be holy. We need to learn how to endure without looking for an escape or shortcut. We want to give up because learning to be holy is hard. Enduring trouble is hard.

Think about the lists we made in the last chapter about what it looks like to be holy. Learning to live and respond with holiness in the *world* takes a lot of practice.

I can talk all day long about how to train to run a race and might even sound like a runner. I can dress in running clothes, show up at races, and post pictures of myself at the start line. But it doesn't make me a runner. In order to be a runner, I have to start running. If I am going to enter a race and make it to the finish line, I have to train for it and endure to the end.

CHAPTER 7: THE TRUTH ABOUT TROUBLE

Let me be honest. I don't like this endurance part.

I get up, get in God's Word, find the direction and strength I need for that day, and make it until about noon. On those days I fall and fail or give up and don't bear up, I beat myself up, seek to escape or try to fix things, I just want the struggle to stop. I decide enough is enough. I'm so often a spiritual wimp. I'd obviously never survive military boot camp. How do they stand there for hours holding a rifle in the air while the rain is pouring down on them? Or how do they sit for hours in freezing cold water and dressed in full battle gear? How do they push themselves physically through those obstacle courses? Why do they do it?

They see the value in being a soldier. To become a soldier, they must endure the training. There are no other options, and there are no short-cuts. Come on now, you know this will preach.

I obviously keep forgetting that God's boot camp for us is trouble.

We are going to experience troubles. No way around this one, and there are no short-cuts. We have two options. Endure or bail. If we are going to be holy then we must endure the training it takes to be made holy. We learn to stand with our hands and hearts raised high while trouble rains on us. We learn to endure extremes of trouble and how to push ourselves mentally and physically through the obstacles of troubles.

God has given us everything we need to be holy. Now we train to be holy. God uses troubles to teach us endurance because endurance is what we need to get us to the finish line of holiness in this life.

Tie it back into James 1:2-4 which says endurance has its perfect result…complete, lacking nothing. If, in faith, we will endure, remain under without looking for an escape or shortcut, trouble can be our holy training.

Before we read these next verses, let me share that Hebrews 11 is called the "faith" chapter. In verses 1-35(a) we learn of the people who accomplished what we would call mighty, miraculous acts in God's power and name (Moses, Joseph, David). These people show us what it looks like to walk out our faith, or to run and finish well our race, as well as God's faithfulness. (Make a mental note that Joseph is mentioned in Hebrews 11 as we'll talk about Joseph later.) Now, fast forward to the end of chapter 11.

Read Hebrews 11:35(b)-38

³⁵...others were tortured, not accepting their release, so that they might obtain a better resurrection; ³⁶and others experienced mockings and scourgings, yes, also chains and imprisonment. ³⁷They were stoned, they were sawn in two, they were tempted, they were put to death with the sword; they went about in sheepskins, in goatskins, being destitute, afflicted, ill-treated ³⁸(men of whom the world was not worthy), wandering in deserts and mountains and caves and holes in the ground.

As we continue to read from Hebrews, let's watch for and mark a few words. They are listed below and above the Scripture reference.

Draw a **jagged line** through references to **endurance**.
Draw a **box** around references to **sin**.

Read Hebrews 12:1

Therefore, since we have so great a cloud of witnesses surrounding us, let us also lay aside every encumbrance and the sin which so easily entangles us, and let us run with endurance the race that is set before us…

- Read the insight box concerning **endurance**.
- Refer to back to Hebrews 11:35(b)-38. What did these people of faith have to endure?

Endurance/Endure
(Hupomone 5281) in the original language means to persevere, remain under. A bearing up under, patience, endurance as to things or circumstances.

Zodhiates, Spiros: *The Complete Word Study Dictionary: New Testament*, electronic ed. Chattanooga, TN: AMG Publishers, ©1992, 1993, and 2000, Strongs G5281

The beloved children of God mentioned in Hebrews 11:35-38, endured things I pray we never must endure. Those who endured much suffering and pain are among those in the cloud of witnesses mentioned in Hebrews 12:1. They are included in Hebrews 11 (the faith chapter) together with those who accomplished what we would call mighty, miraculous acts in God's power and name. That's the kind of relationship and faith experience I want. The kind of relationship and faith that accomplishes mighty, miraculous, acts in God's power and name. The kind of relationship and faith that allows me to endure mocking, scourging, chains, imprisonment, being stoned, sawn in half, tempted, put to death with a sword, destitute, afflicted, ill-treated, and wandering. This level of faith requires endurance. I need to learn to endure.

- According to Hebrews 12:1,

    You are instructed to run with what?

    What will keep you from running your race with endurance?

    What are you instructed to do regarding sin?

Put a **cross** through ***Jesus***.
Draw a **jagged line** through references to ***endured***.
Draw a **box** around ***sin*** and ***sinners***.

Read Hebrews 12:2-4

²fixing our eyes on Jesus, the author and perfecter of faith, who for the joy set before Him endured the cross, despising the shame, and has sat down at the right hand of the throne of God. ³For consider Him who has endured such hostility by sinners against Himself, so that you will not grow weary and lose heart. ⁴You have not yet resisted to the point of shedding blood in your striving against sin;

- How does fixing your eyes on your personal and intimate relationship with Jesus, considering Jesus and what He endured, help you endure or resist, lay aside, or strive against your sin or unholy behavior?

SELF-TALK: Change your mind, change your life

Draw a jagged line through references to **endure**.
Draw a squiggly line underneath references to **discipline**.

Read Hebrews 12:7-13

⁷It is for discipline that you endure; God deals with you as with sons; for what son is there whom his father does not discipline? ⁸But if you are without discipline, of which all have become partakers, then you are illegitimate children and not sons. ⁹Furthermore, we had earthly fathers to discipline us, and we respected them; shall we not much rather be subject to the Father of spirits, and live? ¹⁰For they disciplined us for a short time as seemed best to them, but He disciplines us for our good, so that we may share His holiness. ¹¹All discipline for the moment seems not to be joyful, but sorrowful; yet to those who have been trained by it, afterwards it yields the peaceful fruit of righteousness. ¹²Therefore, strengthen the hands that are weak and the knees that are feeble, ¹³and make straight paths for your feet, so that the limb which is lame may not be put out of joint, but rather be healed.

Discipline (Paideia 3811) in the original language means the whole training and education of children (which relates to the cultivation of mind and morals, and employs for this purpose now commands and admonitions, now reproof and punishment). It also includes the training and care of the body.

Thayer and Smith. Greek Lexicon entry for Peripateo. The NAS New Testament Greek Lexicon 1999

- Read the insight box concerning **discipline**.
- Based on Hebrews 12:7-13, what do you learn about discipline?

- Just to make sure you don't miss it, write out verses 10 and 11 below.

Read Hebrews 12:7 (NIV)

Endure hardship as discipline.

Let's tie Hebrews 12:7 and James 1:2-4 into what I said about training for a race, the example I gave of a woman running in a race, and military boot camp. God uses our various trials and circumstances to train us to be holy. Our training can feel just like that runner who is training and facing horrible weather conditions. Or maybe it can feel like that soldier in boot camp who is day after day pushed to the point of breaking.

We can be tired of training and the discipline required, and might even want to give up. But if we do not endure the training, then we'll never get to the finish line of being holy in our behavior as beloved children of God. If we don't survive boot camp training, we'll never learn to endure when greater tests of our faith come. Trouble is a part of life in this *world* and God uses that trouble to test and prove our faith. This is the good that the *world* needs to see.

If someone has betrayed me, rejected me, or hurt me in any way, it's painful. But to walk in holiness means I am to forgive. To endure during trials means I have to do the right thing every day. On those days or weeks when I've had little to no sleep, everyone needs me, I have nothing left to give, and those around me are on my last nerve, I am to walk in gentleness, kindness, and patience. Do you see where I'm going with this?

We must live out those godly behaviors listed in Chapter 6 while being wronged, suffering injustice, or under great pressure. It is developed and learned. Yes, you and I must endure. We must lay aside every encumbrance and the sin that so easily entangles us.

Knowing how holy looks, or making a list of holy behaviors, is the easy part. Becoming holy is a process. Trouble trains us. Endure the training.

Oh, and fixing our eyes on Jesus reminds us why learning to be holy is so important. Being holy is not only God's will for our lives, but He gives us all we need to be holy. It's all good. Search for it, look for it, anticipate it, and wait for it…

God works for good the trouble meant for evil

According to today's statistics, if four of you are reading this, then at least one of you has been sexually abused. The reality is that we live in a *world* where statistics prove bad, awful, horrible, and perhaps unspeakable things have happened to you, and to those you love. I pray we have found answers together in God's Word for why such evil exists in the *world,* but living with the impact evil has on lives is far more complicated and complex than I am trained or equipped to address.

Even though we have discovered together why trouble and evil exists, the pain and hurt you have experienced is real, deep, and it has certainly shaped your thinking. That's why being mentally prepared and learning how to mentally manage trouble is important. The truth from God's Word about trouble is life-changing. Truth will steady our emotions, bring healing, and dispel lies.

So please, if hurt and pain caused by troubles or evil have paralyzed you, let me encourage you to find good, godly, trained, and professional counsel to help you work through those troubles. At the same time, keep reading the Bible, and as you read, write in a notebook all the relationships you see between people and God. Note how they respond to God in times of troubles and the evil done against them. Also note what they know about God, and what they say about Him during their troubles. What you will find are people who have a deep sense of awe and wonder in God.

Ask God to help you know Him and understand His ways just as they did and experience the same personal relationship with Him. Please do not let your hurt, what you have heard, what you think you know, or those swirling thoughts in your head keep you from knowing what God says about you and the truth about your trouble.

Here is an example of how God used for good, things meant for evil.

In Genesis 37-50, we find the exciting, but trouble-filled story of Joseph. Joseph was the son of Jacob (Israel) whose 12 sons were the 12 tribes of Israel. (Just a reminder that Joseph's name showed up in the faith chapter of Hebrews 11 as an example of one who "endured.")

According to Genesis 37, when Joseph was 17 years old, he had a dream about his life, but it turned out to be more like a nightmare. He dreamed he was ruling over his brothers. When he told them about his dream, they threw him into a pit and left him for dead. Yes, his brothers. But they had second thoughts and decided instead to sell him into slavery.

- Has anyone in your family wanted to kill you or sell you into slavery?

- Has someone else tried to do similar things to you?

- What about emotional destruction, abuse, or bondage?

Fast forward to Genesis 39, and we find Joseph is serving as a slave to an officer of the king of Egypt. Genesis 39:3 and 23 tell us that the Lord was with him and caused all he did to prosper. The Lord was with Joseph, so he became a successful man. Sounds good, you say? Don't forget; he was still a slave in a foreign land.

- Have you ever been in a similar situation where things in one area of your life were horrible but other things were going well?

As it turns out, Joseph was also handsome. His master's wife took a liking to Joseph, but because he refused her attentions, she accused him of trying to take advantage of her. He was imprisoned.

- Have you ever been falsely accused of something and imprisoned?

In return for interpreting their dreams, Joseph asked that they remember him before the king of Egypt. The cupbearer was restored to his office, but the baker was hanged. Yet the cupbearer did not remember Joseph but forgot him.

- Have you ever been forgotten? Or wondered, "Where are you God?" or "Why is God letting all of this happen?"

Fast forward two years and we learn the king of Egypt had a dream. Finally, the cupbearer remembered and told the king about Joseph. Joseph interpreted the meaning of the dream to the king as seven years of abundance in the land followed by seven years of famine in the land. Joseph also told the king how to prepare for the famine. So the king set Joseph over all the land of Egypt. At this point we are in Genesis 41:46, and we learn that Joseph is 30 years old, which meant he spent 13 years as a slave. He had a "nice job" serving a king and being over all the land of Egypt, but still a slave. Sold into slavery by his brothers was not how Joseph dreamed his life would be.

In Genesis 41:50-52, we are told that before the year of famine came, two sons were born to Joseph. The firstborn was named Manasseh meaning, "God has made me forget all my trouble and all my father's household." And the second was named Ephraim meaning, "God has made me fruitful in the land of my affliction." Blessings were amid trouble and affliction. Isn't this interesting and so accurately a picture of life in this crazy *world*? Happiness mixed in with troubles. Thank God for the sprinkled moments of birth, celebration, laughter…happiness.

- Like Joseph, has God made you forget your troubles or made you fruitful during your afflictions?

- What in Joseph's life is similar to your life (trouble, evil done against you, injustice, etc.)?

At the beginning of Chapter 43, we learned the famine was severe, so at least the seven years of abundance had passed and some years of famine. Since we do not know how many years of famine have passed, let's just say Joseph would be between 36 and 44 years old. Guess who heard there was grain in Egypt? Joseph's father. He decided to send Joseph's brothers to Egypt to buy grain. Now just imagine the same brothers who threw you into the pit for dead at 17 but changed their minds and sold you into slavery show up some 19 to 27 years later to buy grain from you.

- How forgiving, kind, and gracious would you be? Would you act, respond, or be holy?

Here is the truth that Joseph knew about God and which changed his mind about his troubles. It's the truth we need to know about God and troubles.

Read Genesis 50:20

As for you, you meant evil against me, but God meant it for good in order to bring about this present result, to preserve many people alive.

- What does Joseph say about what was meant for evil against him?

- What is the truth about what is meant for evil against you?

- What or who are you going to believe about the evil and trouble in your life?

Remember, if you are hurting and in need of healing from the trauma of evil done against you, seek professional and godly counsel. At the same time, take your questions to God. Open His Word and ask Him to answer your questions. Remember, you are pursuing a personal and intimate relationship with Him. Please take God at His Word which says what is meant for evil against you, He means for good. Cling to Him and search for Him. Search for the good.

Look for it, anticipate it and please, wait for it…

Trouble testifies of God's goodness

As I sit here looking back over the lists of ungodly and *world*ly behaviors we made in Chapter 6, I see immorality, greed, filthiness, deception, stealing, evil desires, slander, anger, bitterness, wrath... There is a whole lot of trouble that happens in the *world* because of the things on those lists. Horrible people and things that fill the *world* with hurting people, us included.

> **What better way to show the world the goodness of the Lord than through our troubles? We have all we need (the Word of God and the Spirit of God) to imitate God as we put feet to our faith, walk in this world, and endure our troubles—holy in truth. We have the privilege of showing the world the goodness of God while suffering troubles.**

Sin causes all kinds of trouble, and without Jesus, we are all helpless to do anything about our sin problem. The good news is Jesus, and we have good news to share with and show the *world* about Jesus.

As my sweet mother used to say: "*Put feet to your faith.*"

Meaning your faith is meant to be lived and walked out. Faith is not something you just talk about. Faith is something that is lived and walked out for the *world* to see.

What better way to show the *world* the goodness of the Lord than through our troubles? We have all we need (the Word of God and the Spirit of God) to imitate God as we put feet to our faith, walk in this *world*, and endure our troubles—holy in truth. We have the privilege of showing the *world* the goodness of God while suffering troubles.

Here are just some of the things that come to mind when I think of God and His goodness shown to us:

- Loving
- Compassionate
- Patient
- Truthful
- Forgiving
- Gentle and kind
- Encourages and builds us up

CHAPTER 7: THE TRUTH ABOUT TROUBLE

Just writing this list leaves me in awe and wonder of God. As His beloved children, what a privilege we have to imitate Him by showing the *world* goodness—especially when enduring trouble. Because of our relationship and because we have God's Word and the Holy Spirit of God, we can be:

- Loving when unloved
- Compassionate when being shown no compassion
- Patient rather than impatient
- Truthful and not lie
- Forgiving when hurt
- Gentle and kind when treated harshly and unkindly
- Encourage and build others up rather than discourage and tear others down.

While God has given us everything we need to be holy, we must choose to be holy. The Spirit of God doesn't force us to learn or make us holy robots. We don't get kicked out of God's holiness boot camp—we opt out. How we behave flows out of our desire to be holy. Why? Because we have a growing relationship with Jesus through the Word of God and the teaching and guiding of the Holy Spirit.

Remember, we learn to be holy, which means we aren't going to get it right 100% of the time. Since in this *world* we will have troubles, we are obviously going to get lots of practice. And guess what? It takes a lot of practice and endurance. However, we have the privilege and the ability to imitate God, which means the more we practice, the better we should become at being holy from the heart. In being made holy, you can greatly rejoice. *Joy* can jump! Remember the movie *Inside Out*? *Joy* and *Sadness* are a team!

God takes the broken pieces of our lives caused by troubles and suffering and recycles them into something good for the *world* to see.

Look back through the beautiful description in the Appendix on pages 167-168, or review the lists we made in Chapter 6 of what it looks like to be holy. See good. See holy. See God. This is what the *world* needs to see.

Our godly behavior during times of trouble testifies to the *world* that God is good and works all things together for good for those who love Him. Search for it, look for it, anticipate it and wait for it…

#8 Prepare Your Mind for Action

Remember, return, grow up and stand firm

What an amazing adventure we've taken together through the pages of this book! I say that because writing this book has been an amazing adventure with the Lord for me. I've rediscovered long-forgotten truths and been challenged by new ones.

At times the truth about this crazy *world* is still a hard one for me to grasp, but when I get a grip on the strong bar of truth, I remember there is a liar, liar (the devil). It is so good to no longer be in the dark about what's going on in the *world*. What a blessing to no longer be devoid of truth.

Learning to replace our self-talk with God-talk is a process. But, living in the light of God's Word prepares our minds for action. It gives us courage and brings us in community with others who have prepared their minds for action. What a beautiful and glorious thing to behold. See the description in the Appendix on pages 167-168.

> *Learning to replace our self-talk with God-talk is a process. But, living in the light of God's Word prepares our minds for action. It gives us courage and brings us in community with others who have prepared their minds for action. What a beautiful and glorious thing to behold.*

God redeemed us with the blood of Jesus from our futile (devoid of truth) way of life. He sealed us with His Holy Spirit who abides in us, teaches us, and guides us. As we set ourselves apart in truth, we are given the ability and privilege of being in the *world* to imitate and learn to act like God. Hit the pause button. Our God even takes our troubles and the evil done to us and turns them into good. Who can do that but our God?

Some days your mind will be clear and sharp and filled with truth, and you will act and walk in truth. Some days you'll get blindsided, and that old default self-talk will come flooding in out of nowhere. When it does, and before long, the emotional characters in your head will be running around crazy again. You'll forget. It could be days or weeks before you remember you made a list of God-talk to replace that old, default self-talk. When you realize it, you will start beating yourself up for forgetting. You will tell yourself that you will never get it right. Stop it! This is crazy talk!

Unless Jesus comes for you soon, you will have thousands of opportunities to act in kindness or show patience and forgiveness, and you may or may not extend them. You can decide not to be holy or not to imitate God, but rather to give in to the desire of your flesh and mind. You will learn that you must train your body and your mind to learn how to walk and act according to truth.

Picture in your mind a baby learning to walk. Just as a baby learns to walk, you too will learn to walk in the Spirit. There are going to be times when your walk is not pretty, and when you will fall down or fall short. Fail. Sin.

You cannot give up. You must not give up. You must get up and keep going. Keep training. No matter how many times you fall or how tired you get, keep getting up and keep going. You must learn how to walk by the Spirit. I know it's hard, but here's your motivation.

Remember the blood of Jesus

I've mentioned several times that we must keep Scripture in context. Let me give you a beautiful example of why it is so important. Remember when we discovered truths about this *world* and learned from Revelation there was a war in heaven? The devil and his angels were thrown down and deceived the whole *world*. Let's look at the verses that immediately follow.

Read Revelation 12:7-12

⁷And there was war in heaven, Michael and his angels waging war with the dragon. The dragon and his angels waged war, ⁸and they were not strong enough, and there was no longer a place found for them in heaven. ⁹And the great dragon was thrown down, the serpent of old who is called the devil and Satan, who deceives the whole world; he was thrown down to the earth, and his angels were thrown down with him. ¹⁰Then I heard a loud voice in heaven, saying, "Now the salvation, and the power, and the kingdom of our God and the authority of His Christ have come, for the accuser of our brethren has been thrown down, he who accuses them before our God day and night. ¹¹And they overcame him because of the blood of the Lamb and because of the word of their testimony, and they did not love their life even when faced with death. ¹² For this reason, rejoice, O heavens and you who dwell in them. Woe to the earth and the sea, because the devil has come down to you, having great wrath, knowing that he has only a short time."

- According to verse 11, how did the brethren overcome the devil?

- Based on verse 12, what does the devil have and what does he know?

> **Stay on the alert. The devil is angry because he knows his time is short. He schemes to deceive you. You and I overcome him because of the blood of the Lamb and because of the word of our testimony.**

Stay on the alert. The devil is angry because he knows his time is short. He schemes to deceive you. You and I overcome him because of the blood of the Lamb and because of the word of our testimony. We do not "love our life" even when faced with death. Remember the blood of Jesus and let it compel and motivate us to keep on keeping on. Let us live holy lives in word and deed even when it costs us everything.

- How and why does remembering the blood of Jesus compel and motivate you?

SELF-TALK: Change your mind, change your life

Read 1 Peter 1:13-19

¹³Therefore, prepare your minds for action, keep sober in spirit, fix your hope completely on the grace to be brought to you at the revelation of Jesus Christ. ¹⁴As obedient children, do not be conformed to the former lusts which were yours in your ignorance, ¹⁵but like the Holy One who called you, be holy yourselves also in all your behavior; ¹⁶because it is written, "YOU SHALL BE HOLY, FOR I AM HOLY." ¹⁷If you address as Father the One who impartially judges according to each one's work, conduct yourselves in fear during the time of your stay on earth; ¹⁸knowing that you were not redeemed with perishable things like silver or gold from your futile way of life inherited from your forefathers, ¹⁹but with precious blood, as of a lamb unblemished and spotless, the blood of Christ.

Fear (Phobos 5401) in the original language in the moral sense means reverence, respect or honor.

Zodhiates, Spiros: *The Complete Word Study Dictionary: New Testament*, electronic ed. Chattanooga, TN: AMG Publishers, ©1992, 1993, and 2000, Strongs G5401

- What relationship is described in this passage of Scripture?

- According to verse 13, what three things are you instructed to do?

- According to the first three words in verse 14, why are you to do these three things?

- As an obedient child, what are you to do based on verse 14?

- Based on verse 15, what is the contrast from verse 14 or how is all your behavior to be?

- Read the insight box concerning **fear**.

- According to verse 17, how are you to conduct yourself during the time of your stay on earth?

CHAPTER 8: PREPARE YOUR MIND FOR ACTION

- As a beloved child of God, is being holy a burden or a privilege?

- According to verses 18-19, what motivates you to conduct yourself with reverence, respect, and honor?

- Read the insight box concerning **futile**.
- According to verses 18-19, how is it that you are no longer devoid of truth, etc.?

- Write out what motivates you to do what you are instructed to do in verses 13-17.

Futile (Mataios 3152) in the original language means devoid of truth, vain, empty, fruitless, aimless, useless, no purpose.

Zodhiates, Spiros: The Complete Word Study Dictionary: New Testament, electronic ed. Chattanooga, TN: AMG Publishers, ©1992, 1993, and 2000, Strong G3152

Thayer and Smith. Greek Lexicon entry for Peripateo. The NAS New Testament Greek Lexicon 1999.

As beloved children of God, you and I are no longer devoid of truth. Yes, I'm repeating myself because I need to keep reminding myself. We have the Word of God and the Spirit of God. Remember that the blood of Jesus has redeemed you from your former life devoid of truth and dead in sin. For that reason, you can prepare your mind for action, keep sober in spirit, and fix your hope in Christ. In addition, you must not be conformed to the *world* but be holy and act in reverence, respect, and in awe of God. Remember the blood of Jesus.

Let that precious truth motivate you and fill you with reverence, respect, and awe of God. If it doesn't, you are in trouble. I'm serious. You are in trouble. Get help. Don't isolate yourself. Start re-reading this book and get in THE book, the manual of God's Word. Somewhere your thinking and self-talk are off. Trust me; it can and will happen. That's why this chapter was written. You will want to give in, give up, and hide. But remember there is a liar, liar (the devil).

Get a grip on the strong bar of truth. If you can't get a grip, then find someone who has a grip that can help you. Your adversary is angry that his time is short. In wrath, he seeks to devour you and rob you of truth. He wants to devour your faith.

> **7 AM REMINDER**
> I have been redeemed with the precious blood of Jesus from my ungodly, devoid-of-truth, and helpless-to-do-anything-about-it way of life!

You should remind yourself daily that you have been redeemed with the precious blood of Jesus from your ungodly, devoid-of-truth, and helpless-to-do-anything-about-it way of life. Set this truth as a 7 am daily reminder. Take that time daily to remember the blood of Jesus shed for you. Don't let the *world*, the things of the *world*, and the desires of your flesh and mind rob you of holy life *IN* Christ. You do not want to be robbed of the life He purchased for you and is available to you.

Again, If that daily reminder becomes ho-hum, you are in trouble. If remembering the blood doesn't fill your mind and heart with reverence, awe, wonder, and gratitude, and if it does not motivate you to walk in holiness, then lies have infiltrated your mind. Therefore your mind is not prepared for action.

Remembering the blood of Jesus can keep you focused and single-minded. As such, you are prepared for action.

Return, resist, humble yourself

Read James 4:4-10

> [4]*You adulteresses, do you not know that friendship with the world is hostility toward God? Therefore, whoever wishes to be a friend of the world makes himself an enemy of God.* [5]*Or do you think that the Scripture speaks to no purpose: "He jealously desires the Spirit which He has made to dwell in us"?* [6]*But He gives a greater grace. Therefore, it says, "GOD IS OPPOSED TO THE PROUD, BUT GIVES GRACE TO THE HUMBLE."* [7]*Submit therefore to God. Resist the devil and he will flee from you.* [8]*Draw near to God and He will draw near to you. Cleanse your hands, you sinners; and purify your hearts, you double-minded.* [9]*Be miserable and mourn and weep; let your laughter be turned into mourning and your joy to gloom.* [10]*Humble yourselves in the presence of the Lord, and He will exalt you.*

Tie this verse into what we just looked at in 1 Peter 1:14 on page 148. When, as children of God, we conform to our former lusts, we are walking according to the *world*. We act like we are devoid of truth. We behave like the *world*—unholy. God calls this "friendship with the *world*." The bottom-line is this is spiritual adultery. It's sin.

Our acting like the *world* is hostility toward God. Well, if we were in our right minds, single-minded, and prepared for action, we'd never cheat on God. Not after what He has done for us so we can be in

CHAPTER 8: PREPARE YOUR MIND FOR ACTION

relationship with Him. We'd never want to be called or considered a friend of the *world* whose ruler is the devil. Friendship with the *world* makes us an enemy of God. What are we thinking? Exactly! We obviously aren't thinking. So how does this passage help us understand what is going on and how to prepare our minds? How do we make sure it doesn't happen or what to do when it does happen?

- Read the insight box concerning **proud** and **double-minded**.
- According to verse 6 and the last word in 8, what is the root or cause of this spiritual adultery?

- Just so you make sure you understand what's happening to you, using the definition of proud and double-minded, explain how being proud and double-minded in your thinking and actions makes you friendly with the *world*. Or as 1 Peter 1:14 says, what happens when you conform to your former lusts.

- According to these verses, is being proud and double-minded sin against God?

- Based on verses 7-8, what are we to do when we realize we've sinned against God?

- Based on verses 7-8, how does God say He will respond to you if you do what He says to do?

Proud (Huperephanos 5244) in the original language means arrogant, proud. Often associated with the rejection of God.

Double-minded (Dipsuchos 1374) in the original language means such a person suffers from divided loyalties. On the one hand, he wishes to maintain a religious confession and desires the presence of God in his life; on the other hand, he loves the ways of the *world* and prefers to live according to its mores and ethics.

Zodhiates, Spiros: *The Complete Word Study Dictionary: New Testament,* electronic ed. Chattanooga, TN: AMG Publishers, ©1992, 1993, and 2000, Strongs G5244 and G1347

> **When we get friendly with the world and sin, God wants us to submit ourselves to Him. Do you see how kind and gentle and gracious God is with us? He tells us to draw near to Him (rather than near to the world), and He will draw near to us.**

When we get friendly with the *world* and sin, God wants us to submit ourselves to Him. Do you see how kind and gentle and gracious God is with us? He tells us to draw near to Him (rather than near to the *world*), and He will draw near to us. He loves us so much that He wants us to return to him with a pure and humble heart—to repent in sorrow for our sin against Him. Give up your right to think and act based on what you think is right. In fact, give up all your rights. He says in doing this, He will exalt you.

Do you know what that word exalt means? It means dignity and honor. Oh, the emotional character of *Shame* must shut up and sit down in the face of that truth. I cannot tell you I fully get my mind around the ways of God, but He says that if we confess and repent of our sin and humble ourselves in His presence, He will bestow dignity and honor on us. Period.

I don't know why I would ever be friendly with the *world*, but I am guilty of committing spiritual adultery. It breaks my heart as I know I have broken the heart of God. I get distracted by the things and ways of the *world*. Things catch my eye, draw my attention, and seemingly satisfy some desire, longing, or need. As my mind fixes on the things and ways of the *world*, then I begin to think on them. Soon my behavior follows. There I go imitating the *world* rather than imitating God.

The old saying, "if it looks like a duck, swims like a duck, and quacks like a duck, then it probably is a duck," is true. If we look like the *world*, and behave like the *world*, and talk like the *world*, then we've conformed to the *world*.

Listen up. You and I can never allow the *world* to shape how we think, and what we believe and do, because the *world* is hostile to God. Can you tell me why?

- Based on all we've discovered, write out below why the *world* is hostile to God.

CHAPTER 8: PREPARE YOUR MIND FOR ACTION

I pray, pray, pray, that you wrote that we could never allow the *world* to shape what we think, believe, and do because the ruler of this *world* is the devil. The devil is a liar, a murderer, and has been from the beginning. He prowls around looking for someone to devour, there is no truth in him, and he deceives the whole *world*. Further, those in the *world* and without Jesus are all devoid of the truth.

- Ask the Lord to show you specific ways you are imitating the *world* and being friendly with the *world*. He will graciously and lovingly show you. When He does, repent and humble yourself. Don't beat yourself up. Don't convince yourself you can't do this holy life. Don't say you can't forgive yourself or tell yourself it's just too hard. God-talk overrides your self-talk.

Read 1 John 1:9

If we confess our sins, He is faithful and righteous to forgive us our sins and to cleanse us from all unrighteousness.

Read Psalm 103:12

As far as the east is from the west, so far has He removed our transgressions from us.

- According to 1 John 1:9,

  When you confess your sin to God, what does God say He will do concerning your sin?

  Does this truth apply to every sin you confess to Him?

  What are you to do every time you sin?

  What will God do every time you confess your sin?

  No matter what you tell yourself, what is the truth about the confessing of your sin and receiving God's forgiveness?

- According to Psalm 103:12, how far has God removed your sins from you?

- How far is the east from the west?

- If you have confessed and repented of your sin, God says He forgives that sin and then removes that sin from you as far as the east is from the west. So why do you keep thinking about it, bringing it up, beating yourself up, and telling yourself that you can't forgive yourself? Is that thinking in opposition to God's Word, truth?

There can be aftermath and consequences of sin, and maybe even retribution that can sure make it hard to forget the foolishness of our sin. But God gives strength and grace to endure during these times, too. His forgiveness gives us the ability to walk in humility with dignity and honor—free of guilt and shame. Read James 4:4-10 (page 150).

Prepare your mind for action! Remember that the blood of Jesus has redeemed you from your futile way of life (and thinking). Come to your senses, return (submit and repent), resist the devil, draw near to God and He will draw near to you. Humble yourself before the Lord and he will exalt you. Not *if*, but when you fall, fail, or sin, get up, repent, and keep walking in holiness.

Grow up

The book of Ephesians was written to and for a group of people who also lived in an evil culture and in the *world*. They were involved in all kinds of evil practices, but had been redeemed with the blood of Jesus. They were the very first Christians in their city.

Praise God, they were no longer devoid of truth. As such, they gave up their evil and unholy practices and lifestyle. For some, this drastic change in lifestyle may have meant losing jobs or severing relationships with family and friends. They suffered and endured because of their priority relationship with Jesus.

These new Christians learned by the Word of God, through the Spirit of God, how to be holy and walk in the Spirit of Truth. They sorted through old patterns of thinking and desires of the flesh. At the same time, they were living in a culture opposed to God and were undergoing dramatic and supernatural changes in behavior. Does any of this sound familiar?

Because they were the first Christians, they had *few* living examples of what it looked like to be a Christ follower or how to imitate God. Interestingly, some of the lists we made in Chapter 6 were from Ephesians. Paul wrote the book of Ephesians. He is the one that shared the gospel with these precious people. He spent several

CHAPTER 8: PREPARE YOUR MIND FOR ACTION

years with them teaching them and showing them what it meant to be a Christ follower. Because Paul was no longer there, he wrote a letter of encouragement and instruction. Paul understood the difficultly of living in a culture and *world* opposed to God.

In the book of Ephesians Paul takes the first two chapters to remind the Ephesians of who they are in Christ and who they were before Christ. It's the reminder we all need to fill our minds with truth. In Ephesians 1:7, Paul reminds them that they have been redeemed by the blood of Jesus. Then, later in the book, Paul has a "therefore" coming. The word "therefore" is a summary statement. Paul is saying, because of everything I have just told you…because of who you are in Christ…because of what is true about you in Christ… He says in Ephesians 4:1, "Therefore, walk in a manner worthy" and in 5:1, "Therefore, be imitators of God as beloved children." Paul is reminding them and motivating them to be holy in an unholy *world*.

In showing them what it looks like to walk holy in their *world*, or walk in a manner worthy, Paul also talks to them about (1) the body of Christ (or the church) and the purpose of the church, and (2) putting on the armor of God.

Let's read this passage of Scripture about the church, and then let's break it down.

Read Ephesians 4:11-24

11And He (Jesus) gave some as apostles, and some as prophets, and some as evangelists, and some as pastors and teachers, 12for the equipping of the saints for the work of service, to the building up of the body of Christ; 13until we all attain to the unity of the faith, and of the knowledge of the Son of God, to a mature man, to the measure of the stature which belongs to the fullness of Christ. 14As a result, we are no longer to be children, tossed here and there by waves and carried about by every wind of doctrine, by the trickery of men, by craftiness in deceitful scheming; 15but speaking the truth in love, we are to grow up in all aspects into Him who is the head, even Christ, 16from whom the whole body, being fitted and held together by what every joint supplies, according to the proper working of each individual part, causes the growth of the body for the building up of itself in love. 17So this I say, and affirm together with the Lord, that you walk no longer just as the Gentiles also walk, in the futility of their mind, 18being darkened in their understanding, excluded from the life of God because of the ignorance that is in them, because of the hardness of their heart; 19and they, having become callous, have given themselves over to sensuality for the practice of every kind of impurity with greediness. 20But you did not learn Christ in this way, 21if indeed you have heard Him and have been taught in Him, just as truth is in Jesus, 22that, in reference to your former manner of life, you lay aside the old self, which is being corrupted in accordance with the lusts of deceit, 23and that you be renewed in the spirit of your mind, 24and put on the new self, which in the likeness of God has been created in righteousness and holiness of the truth.

- Based on verse 17, how are you are to **no** longer walk?

- Based on all you have learned so far, how and why is it that you can no longer walk in the futility of your mind, devoid of truth?

- According to verse 22, how is your "old self" described?

- What does verse 23 tell you to do?

- Verse 24 says your new-self is in the likeness of who, and has been created in what?

CHAPTER 8: PREPARE YOUR MIND FOR ACTION

Grow up! But, to mature as a believer, you need help. Let's keep breaking down this passage of Scripture from Ephesians.

Commit to a body of believers

Re-read Ephesians 4:11-14

[11]And He (Jesus) gave some as apostles, and some as prophets, and some as evangelists, and some as pastors and teachers, [12]for the equipping of the saints for the work of service, to the building up of the body of Christ; [13]until we all attain to the unity of the faith, and of the knowledge of the Son of God, to a mature man, to the measure of the stature which belongs to the fullness of Christ. [14]As a result, we are no longer to be children, tossed here and there by waves and carried about by every wind of doctrine, by the trickery of men, by craftiness in deceitful scheming;

- According to verse 11, what did Jesus give?

- Based on verses 12-13, why did Jesus give apostles, prophets, evangelists, pastors, and teachers?

- What will be the result based on verse 14?

I wasn't sure what sub-title to give this section. Should I say join a church, go to church, find a tribe, connect with a body of believers? Here's the point. Find a group of people who follow Christ (not a building). Connect with them, commit to them, dig in, plant yourself there, grow, and serve. I know it's a huge risk. Yes, it's "peoplely" out there. God-talk yourself through this one.

Pray and ask the Lord to show you where there is a Bible-believing, Bible-teaching body of believers where you can mature and grow up in all aspects of Christ as well as serve.

Don't get upset, whine, and give up when people in the church act unholy. You know when they act unkind, unloving, gossip, are impatient and so on. You aren't going to get it right 100% of the time either. Understand that there are no perfect churches because there are no perfect people. You included. That person or those persons causing "trouble" could be your opportunity or test to be holy and show or model holy. Remember?

Go back to the Appendix and read through that beautiful list. Look for people who are pursuing or exhibit those qualities, and when you find them, approach them. Introduce yourself, ask them for their help. Whatever they are doing, ask if you can help them or hang out with them. If they are leading Bible studies, attend them. If they will one-on-one pray with you or teach you God's Word, let them! Then you start looking for others that you can come alongside and do the same thing.

- What is the word picture found in Ephesians 4:14 of a child in the faith, or someone not mature in faith?

If you aren't committed and connected with a body of believers who believe the Word of God is absolute truth, and where you are growing and maturing in your faith, that word picture is you. If you are not growing in truth, you will soon be tossed and carried about by the trickery of men, by craftiness in deceitful scheming. Think about these words: the trickery of men, by craftiness in deceitful scheming. It can even look or seem good. But it's tricky, crafty, deceitful scheming. It's all around you. It's trouble with a capital T. Do not be deceived. You cannot grow in your faith in isolation apart from God's people and God's Word. God-talk yourself through this one. Grow up!

You have been given a spiritual gift

God has made you very uniquely you! He's given you certain abilities, talents, skills, a personality and because of your relationship with Jesus, you are a new you and have been given a spiritual gift or gifts. Not only do you have the Holy Spirit of God teaching, guiding and abiding in you, but you have been given supernatural abilities.

CHAPTER 8: PREPARE YOUR MIND FOR ACTION

Re-read Ephesians 4:11-13

¹¹And He (Jesus) gave some as apostles, and some as prophets, and some as evangelists, and some as pastors and teachers, ¹²for the equipping of the saints for the work of service, to the building up of the body of Christ; ¹³until we all attain to the unity of the faith, and of the knowledge of the Son of God, to a mature man, to the measure of the stature which belongs to the fullness of Christ.

As you can see from Ephesians 4:11-13, some of the gifts are given for the equipping of the saints for the works of service. As you grow in maturity, you'll want to learn more about spiritual gifts so that you can discover how God has uniquely gifted you. 1 Corinthians 12 gives even more, insight into the various spiritual gifts. These gifts are given for the common good. They are meant to be used in service to others. You have superpowers that are to be used for good!

As you start maturing in your faith and serving in your church, you will begin to learn and understand how God has gifted you spiritually. Learning about and developing your spiritual gifts should be done within your church and is why you need to commit to a body of believers so you can grow up.

> *You are part of the body of Christ now. His children, His family, His church. You cannot live, grow and thrive in isolation. Think about it. How dangerous would that be in this world to isolate yourself thinking you didn't need to connect with and commit to other believers.*

You are part of the body of Christ now. His children, His family, His church. You cannot live, grow and thrive in isolation. Think about it. How dangerous would that be in this *world* to isolate yourself thinking you didn't need to connect with and commit to other believers. While you are getting tossed and carried about by the trickery of men or by craftiness in deceitful scheming, your faith is being devoured.

Stand firm

Remember what I shared about the group of believers in Ephesus, their culture, and why Paul was writing to them? Here's how he ends his letter.

Read Ephesians 6:10-17

¹⁰Finally, be strong in the Lord and in the strength of His might. ¹¹Put on the full armor of God, so that you will be able to stand firm against the schemes of the devil. ¹²For our struggle is not against flesh and blood, but against the rulers, against the powers, against the world forces of this darkness, against the spiritual forces of wickedness in the heavenly places. ¹³Therefore, take up the full armor of God, so that you will be able to resist in the evil day, and having done everything, to stand firm. ¹⁴Stand firm therefore, HAVING GIRDED YOUR LOINS WITH TRUTH, and HAVING PUT ON THE BREASTPLATE OF RIGHTEOUSNESS, ¹⁵and having shod YOUR FEET WITH THE PREPARATION OF THE GOSPEL OF PEACE; ¹⁶in addition to all, taking up the shield of faith with which you will be able to extinguish all the flaming arrows of the evil one. ¹⁷And take THE HELMET OF SALVATION, and the sword of the Spirit, which is the word of God.

- What are you instructed to do in verse 10 and how are you to do this?

- According to verse 11, what are you to do so that you can stand firm against the schemes of the devil?

- Based on all we've discovered, what are the schemes of the devil?

- According to verse 12, describe the struggle:

CHAPTER 8: PREPARE YOUR MIND FOR ACTION

Re-read Ephesians 6:13-17

¹³Therefore, take up the full armor of God, so that you will be able to resist in the evil day, and having done everything, to stand firm. ¹⁴Stand firm therefore, HAVING GIRDED YOUR LOINS WITH TRUTH, and HAVING PUT ON THE BREASTPLATE OF RIGHTEOUSNESS, ¹⁵and having shod YOUR FEET WITH THE PREPARATION OF THE GOSPEL OF PEACE; ¹⁶in addition to all, taking up the shield of faith with which you will be able to extinguish all the flaming arrows of the evil one. ¹⁷And take THE HELMET OF SALVATION, and the sword of the Spirit, which is the word of God.

- Based on verses 13-17, what is the full armor of God? List each piece:

- Go back now, and write next to each piece what it does.
- Now, go back and write out what you are to do with the pieces.
- What is your one weapon?

- Taking all the Scriptures we've examined together in this chapter, write out and tell yourself why it is important for you to stand firm and how you are going to stand firm. What's your plan?

Get in, stay in and take up the Word of God

Relationships grow and stay strong because people make the relationship a priority. They give each other full access to their hearts and share from their hearts. They value, honor, and respect each other and the relationship. Your relationship with God is no different. Spending time daily listening to God through the reading or studying of His Word and talking to Him (prayer) is critical to your spiritual, emotional and mental health.

> *Spending time daily listening to God through the reading or studying of His Word and talking to Him (prayer) is critical to your spiritual, emotional and mental health.*

I've gone through periods where I read God's Word and journaled. For years I sat under the teaching of Charles Stanley, and as I marked up my Bible, God marked up my heart. Sometimes I would listen to 2 or 3 of his sermons daily while taking notes. Then, I went through decades of intense inductive Bible study. One year I listened to the Chronological Bible and another year the dramatized Bible. Last year I purchased a coloring Bible and slowly savored Genesis, Exodus, Psalms, and Proverbs. The point is to get in and stay in the Word of God. Here are a few suggestions:

- Attend Bible studies: If your church does not offer Bible studies, ask your pastor how you can start one. Or get a recommendation from your pastor for a community Bible study that you could attend.

  Remember, you are responsible for understanding God's Word for yourself, so make sure not to believe everything you hear or think. Test everything against God's Word, so study hard and keep His Word in context. That means study what comes before and after a passage, and that could mean reading the whole book.

- Listen to God's Word: There are wonderful apps that you can download that allow you to listen to God's Word while you drive, get dressed in the morning, do chores, or at night before going to bed. Try listening to the dramatized versions.

- Read a Proverb a day: As you read, ask God to show you one or two that answer some questions in your heart or speak to some circumstance in your life. When He makes His Word personal to you, praise Him, ask Him to hide it in your heart, and take that Word with you throughout the day.

- When you read using your Bible, mark references to God and Jesus and then list in the margin what you learn about them and ask God to help you to experience these truths personally. Later, as you flip through your Bible, review your lists and how God has answered your prayers.

- Praise and Worship music: On those days when you don't have two brain cells to rub together then turn on the music and turn it up. Let God's Word go in one ear and straight to your heart. Let someone sing truth to you. It's still the truth, and you need it. In fact, turn on the praise music anytime!

- Pray God's Word: Pray the truth over yourself and others. Remember those Proverbs you might be reading each day? Well, as you read and find characteristics you want to develop, stop and ask God to make those things true of you, and while you are at it, ask Him to make them true of those you love. Pray the verse and those specific characteristics over those people by name. There are other wonderful prayers and pleas in Scripture that you can personalize and pray. When you find them, write them down in a notebook or write down the book of the Bible, chapter, and verse (address) so you know where to go to find them again. Pray these verses over yourself and others frequently! Praying God's Word is praying God's will—if you keep the verses in context.

There are so many more things I could share with you, but ask God, ask other believers and try different things. Just stay close to God by getting in and staying in His Word. Remember, you want it to wash over you and clean and change your mind and heart. When you brush your teeth, you expect them to be clean and different. When you bathe you expect to be clean and different. When you go to God's Word, you should expect to be clean and different. Your time in God's Word should fill you with reverence for, and awe and wonder of our Lord. It should strengthen and deepen your personal and intimate relationship with your Heavenly Father.

If you find you are losing the desire to be in God's Word or spend time with God, or if you are leaving your time with Him and are not different, then stop and pray and ask Him to reveal to you what is going on. Seek wise and godly counsel from a mature believer. There could be something going on with you physically. You know what? You might just be tired and need to sleep. God knows, so ask Him because you know that if you go too long without spending time with Him and allowing His Word to wash over your mind, you'll be in trouble.

Rest in this truth.

Read Philippians 1:6

For I am confident of this very thing, that He who began a good work in you will perfect it until the day of Christ Jesus.

Isn't this the most wonderful verse you have ever heard? You are His well-loved child. He loves you with an everlasting love. He redeemed you from your futile way of life with the precious blood of Jesus. He is going to complete the good work He began in you. Rest in this truth. He has you. Just keep pursuing Him, and while you do, He'll do the work in and through you.

> **You are His well-loved child. He loves you with an everlasting love. He redeemed you from your futile way of life with the precious blood of Jesus. He is going to complete the good work He began in you.**

Conclusion

I am so grateful for the opportunity to journey through these pages with you. During the months of writing this book, I've had to God-talk myself through many situations. I admit that my default self-talk has kicked in on more than one occasion. Sometimes I recognized it immediately and other times it was late in the day before I snapped out of it. Sadly, a few daily reminders about the precious blood of Jesus were ignored because I was busy, thought I'd get back to it, but never did. I may not know who you are, but as I have prayed for myself, I have prayed for you. My constant prayer for us comes from Matthew 22:39 which says "…love the Lord your God with all of your heart, and with all your soul, and with all your mind."

> "…love the Lord your God with all of your heart, and with all your soul, and with all your mind."

Oh, that we would love the Lord our God with all of our hearts, and with all of our souls, and with all of our minds. But, how do we do that? Sure, we cry "God help us," but what better way to grow in our love of the Lord our God than to spend time with Him and in His Word.

So what's next? Where do we go from here? I love how Kay Arthur, in her book *His Imprint My Expression: Changed Forever By the Master's Touch*, answers these questions.

> "Do you want an intimate relationship with God? If so, you must set aside time so your heavenly Father can communicate with you through His Word and through His Spirit. Talk with Him in prayer. Put yourself in a position for God to meet with you, and everything else will fall into perspective. You will learn to recognize His voice."

In the last chapter, I gave you a few tips for getting in and staying in God's Word. Ask the Lord if you should pick one or if He has a better idea. In the meantime, let me ask you to consider this next thing.

- Get some paper, your Bible or Bible app, and a pencil or pen.
- Go to Psalm 104.
- Read and mark references to God.
- Make a list of God's wonders in the margin of your Bible or in a notebook..
- Review the list and be in awe.
- Worship.

John 4:23 says we are to worship the Father in spirit and in truth. The word worship here, in the original language, means to "kiss the hand to (towards) one, in token of reverence.[1]"

Beloved child of God, bow low and worship. Blow kisses upward.

I would love to hear from you. If willing, please take a few minutes to give me your feedback by going to my website at https://sallyhhall.com/selftalkfeedback.

I look forward to that day when we are all gathered together and in His presence face to face. I'll get to see your face too. Glory be to God.

Appendix

The most important work you can do is sanctify yourself in the truth and keep on sanctifying yourself until you take your final breath. It won't just happen. You'll need to be focused and intentional. Let God's Word wash over you, cleansing you, and washing away the *world* so that your thinking, values, attitudes and behaviors are holy, so that you walk and work in the *world* holy in truth.

I want you to see what it looks like to be set apart in thinking, values, attitudes and behaviors. I went through God's Word, pulling out only some verses that describe what it looks like to be holy or godly. Much like we did in Chapter 6. I then combined these truths so you could get a bigger picture of what it looks like to be holy and set apart for God in the middle of a crazy *world*.

The below is a beautiful picture of the what it looks like to walk and work in the *world*: holy in truth. This community is possible because its people have a personal and intimate relationship with Jesus and as such have the Word of God and the Spirit of God abiding within. Let me encourage you to find people like this and learn from them. Become like this description. Raise up others to be like this.

A recording of this description can be found at sallyhhall.com.

If you decide to read these verses rather than listen to the recording, read as one long description. Leave out the passage references and read to visualize and imagine. If you are reading this with others, some might consider closing their eyes. Imagine while listening…

A community of people who:

- Have confessed with their mouth Jesus and Lord and believed in their heart God raised Him from the dead. (Romans 10:9-10)
- Received Christ Jesus as Lord and walk in Him. (Colossians 2:6)
- Know they have been redeemed from their futile way of life with the precious blood of Christ. (1 Peter 1:18-19)
- Have been sealed in the Spirit, are taught by the Spirit and live and walk by the Spirit. (Ephesians 1:13; John 14:25-27; Galatians 5:25)
- Glorify God with one mouth. (Romans 15:6)
- Have full assurance of understanding, resulting in a true knowledge of Christ. (Colossians 2:2)
- Trust God and lean not on their own understanding. (Proverbs 3:5)
- Are presented complete in Christ. (Colossians 1:28)
- Admonished and teach with all wisdom. (Colossians 1:28)
- Proclaim God's excellencies. (1 Peter 2:9-10)

- Bear fruit in every good work. (Colossians 1:9-11)
- Grow in true knowledge. (Colossians 1:9-11)
- Are strong with all power according to God's might. (Colossians 1:9-11)
- Are firmly established in the faith. (Colossians 1:23)
- Labor and strive in God's mighty power that works within. (Colossians 1:29)
- Are steadfast, immovable, abound in the work of the Lord. (1 Corinthians 15:58)
- Are firmly rooted and built up in Christ. (Colossians 2:7-8)
- Are established in their faith. (Colossians 2:7-8)
- Have hearts that overflow with gratitude. (Colossians 2:7-8)
- Do nothing from selfishness or empty conceit. (Philippians 2:2-4)
- Have humility of mind. (Philippians 2:2-4)
- Regard others as more important than self. (Philippians 2:2-4)
- Have the same mind, same love. (Philippians 2:2-4)
- Are united in the same spirit and intent on one purpose. (Philippians 2:2-4)
- Fulfill every desire for goodness and the work of faith with power, glorifying God. (2 Thessalonians 1:11-12)
- Are diligent to present themselves approved. (2 Timothy 2:15)
- Are spokesmen who need not be ashamed. (2 Timothy 2:15)
- Handle accurately the word of truth. (2 Timothy 2:15)
- Hold fast the faithful Word. (Titus 1:9)
- Are able to exhort in sound doctrine. (Titus 1:9)
- Do not in folly go astray. (Proverbs 5:23)
- Destroy speculations and every lofty thing raised up against the knowledge of God. (2 Corinthians 10:5)
- Take every thought captive to the obedience of Christ. (2 Corinthians 10:5)
- Are devoted to teaching. (Acts 2:42-47)
- Are filled with awe for God and His Word. (Acts 2:42-47)
- Respect and hold in high regard those who work hard in overseeing and admonishing the community. (1 Thessalonians 5:11-15)
- Live in peace. (1 Thessalonians 5:11-15)
- Are not idle. (1 Thessalonians 5:11-15)
- Encourage the fainthearted and help the weak. (1 Thessalonians 5:11-15)
- Abound with patience. (1 Thessalonians 5:11-15)
- Do not pay back wrong with wrong. (1 Thessalonians 5:11-15)
- Are not conformed to the *world* but are transformed by the renewing of their minds. (Romans 12:2)
- Prove what is the good, acceptable, perfect will of God. (Romans 12:2)
- Speak the things fitting for sound doctrine. (Titus 2:1)
- Are able to teach the next generation. (Psalm 78:1-8)
- Understand that the Word is living and active. (Hebrews 4:12)
- Provide opportunity for the Word to penetrate, divide soul/spirit, joints/marrow. (Hebrews 4:12)

APPENDIX

- Provide opportunity for God's Word to judge thoughts and attitudes of the heart. (Hebrews 4:12)
- Are filled with the knowledge of God's will through all spiritual wisdom and understanding. (Colossians 1:9-11)
- Live lives worthy of God and please Him in every way. (Colossians 1:9-11)
- Experience many wonders and miracles by God's mighty power. (Acts 2:42-47)
- Ensure no one has need.(Acts 2:42-47)
- With passion for God, meet together with glad and sincere hearts. (Acts 2:42-47)
- Enjoy the favor of others. (Acts 2:42-47)
- God adds to their numbers daily those who are being saved. (Acts 2:41, 47)
- Are devoted to one another in love. (Romans 12:10)
- Honor each other. (Romans 12:10)
- Practice hospitality. (Romans 12:13)
- Show hospitality to strangers. (Hebrews 13:2)
- Do not pass judgment on one another. (Romans 14:13)
- Put no stumbling block or obstacle in anyone's way. (Romans 14:13)
- Accept one another as Christ accepted them in order to bring praise to God. (Romans 15:7)
- Put on a heart of compassion, kindness, humility, gentleness, patience, bear with and forgive one another and the peace of Christ rules in hearts. (Colossians 3: 12-13)
- Are completely humble and gentle with each other. (Ephesians 4:2)
- Are patient and bear with one another in love. (Ephesians 4:2)
- Make every effort to keep unity of the Spirit through the bond of peace, building up others. (Romans 14:19, Ephesians 4:3)
- Are kind and tender hearted. (Ephesians 4:32)
- Forgive others. (Ephesians 4:32)
- Are submissive out of reverence for Christ. (Ephesians 5:21)
- Can be trusted with the confession of others and are quick to pray for healing and restoration. (James 5:16)
- Make intercession for others. (James 5:16)
- Help those who wander from the truth. (James 5:19-20)
- Encourage and build each other up. (1 Thessalonians 5:11-15)
- Love each other deeply. (1 Peter 4:8-10)
- Offer hospitality to one another without grumbling. (1 Peter 4:8-10)
- Use their spiritual gifts to serve others. (1 Peter 4:8-10)
- Faithfully administer God's grace. (1 Peter 4:8-10)
- Do not dishonor the Word of God. (Titus 2:3-5)
- Are set apart from the *world* by their behavior. (John 17:17)

Notes

Getting Started
1. sallyhhall.com/resources.

Introduction
1. Paul Trip, "Talking to Yourself," *Wednesday's Word* (blog), March 13, 2013, accessed October 17, 2017, https://www.paultripp.com/wednesdays-word/posts/talking-to-yourself.
2. Docter, Pete, Ronnie Del Carmen, Meg LeFauve, Josh Cooley, Jonas Rivera, Amy Poehler, Phyllis Smith, et al. 2015. *Inside Out*.
3. Free preview of *Inside Out*, accessed, October 17, 2017, http://video.disney.com/watch/free-preview-of-inside-out-523203999f8b331d2506bc36.
4. sallyhhall.com/resources/.
5. Our long-time pastor and teacher, Tim Ackley, explains the heart using this train metaphor. "The mind is the locomotive (beliefs, perspectives, thinking, attitudes, etc.), the feelings the caboose (sends signals to the mind that all is well, or danger!), and the will functions as the tracks that will lead the train to its desired destination. All three must work together and the gospel aims at all of them in transforming power. Otherwise, train wreck, derailment, or traveling into places where there will be harm or danger." Used with permission.

Chapter #1
1. Free preview of *Inside Out*, accessed, October 17, 2017, http://video.disney.com/watch/free-preview-of-inside-out-523203999f8b331d2506bc36.
2. Jack Lim, published on October 9, 2011, "Helen Reddy - I Am Woman (with lyrics)," accessed October 17, 2027, https://youtu.be/V6fHTyVmYp4.
3. cosmic cosmo, published November 30, 2014, "Enjoli – Classic 80/s Commercial, accessed October 17, 2017, https://youtu.be/_UIktO4Pnlw.
4. Barbie. In *Wikipedia*. Accessed October 17, 2017 from https://en.wikipedia.org/wiki/Barbie.
5. Twiggy. In *Wikipedia*. Accessed October 17, 2017 from https://en.wikipedia.org/wiki/Twiggy.
6. Me Generation. In *Wikipedia*. Accessed October 17. 2017 from https://en.wikipedia.org/wiki/Me_generation.
7. Lewis Bunting, "Life is a Roller Coaster," 2012. Accessed October 17, 2017, https://allpoetry.com/poem/9632309-Life-is-Like-a-Rollercoaster-by-Lewis-is-cool.

Chapter #2

1. "Roller Coaster Quotes," Brainy Quotes. Accessed October 17, 2017, https://www.brainyquote.com/quotes/quotes/r/rushlimbau454798.html?src=t_roller_coaster.
2. *Is Genesis History?* https://isgenesishistory.com/a-brief-overview/.
3. American Bible Society, accessed October 17, 2017, http://bibleresources.americanbible.org/resource/a-brief-description-of-popular-bible-translations.
4. Dale Hanson Bourke, *Embracing Your Second Calling: Find Passion and Purpose for the Rest of Your Life*, (Nashville: Thomas Nelson Publishers, 2010), 205.

Chapter #3

1. American Bible Society, bibleresources.americanbible.org, "A Brief Description of Popular Bible Translations", *All Resources, Categories: About the Bible, Translations.* Accessed October 17, 2017, http://bibleresources.americanbible.org/resource/a-brief-description-of-popular-bible-translations.

Chapter #4

1. OTG Ministry, published March 26, 2016, "Jesus on the Cross – A Medical Perspective (viewer discretion)," accessed October 17, 2017, https://youtu.be/ZBHnvPKvK8U.
2. "Jen Wilkin quotes, Author Quotes," Good Reads, accessed October 17. 2017, https://www.goodreads.com/author/quotes/7328168.Jen_Wilkin.
3. "Snatch you bald headed" is southern slang used to express how upset someone is with someone else's behavior.

Chapter #7

1. Pollyannaish, accessed October 17, 2017, http://www.dictionary.com/browse/pollyanna.
2. These were notes written in the margin of my Bible. I do not know where they came from, but evidently were shared during a sermon or teaching or gleaned during a study time. The words impacted me greatly, so I recorded them in my Bible.

Conclusion

1. Thayer and Smith. "Greek Lexicon entry for Proskuneo". "The NAS New Testament Greek Lexicon". 1999. Accessed October 17, 2017, https://www.biblestudytools.com/lexicons/greek/nas/proskuneo.html.

www.ingramcontent.com/pod-product-compliance
Lightning Source LLC
Chambersburg PA
CBHW060459010526
44118CB00018B/2470